Steve —
From Germany and
London – Summer 85.

Love, Marion

CLIVE LLOYD

CLIVE LLOYD

The Authorised Biography

TREVOR MCDONALD

GRANADA
London Toronto Sydney New York

Granada Publishing Limited
8 Grafton Street, London W1X 3LA

Published by Granada Publishing 1985

Copyright © Trevor McDonald 1985

British Library Cataloguing in Publication Data

McDonald, Trevor
  Clive Lloyd : the authorised biography.
  1. Lloyd, Clive   2. Cricket players——
  Guyana——Biography
  I. Title
  796.35'8'0924   GV915.L57

ISBN 0-246-12553-5

Printed by Bell and Bain Ltd., Glasgow
and bound by Hunter and Foulis Ltd., Edinburgh

The lines from T. S. Eliot on p. 1 are reproduced by
permission of Faber and Faber Ltd from *Collected
Poems 1909–1962* by T. S. Eliot.

For Geraldine and Eunice and Jacy

Contents

Preface   xi
Acknowledgements   xiii

CHAPTER ONE	Saluting the Captain	1
CHAPTER TWO	The Beginning	13
CHAPTER THREE	How the Captaincy Evolved	27
CHAPTER FOUR	Learning in Australia – and Elsewhere	40
CHAPTER FIVE	Frustration	49
CHAPTER SIX	'Hubert' Takes Command	62
CHAPTER SEVEN	A New Philosophy Takes Shape	78
CHAPTER EIGHT	The Packer Revolution	90
CHAPTER NINE	England Humiliated	105
CHAPTER TEN	The Apotheosis of Speed	118
CHAPTER ELEVEN	Captain of Champions	130
CHAPTER TWELVE	Bitter-Sweet Finale	146
CHAPTER THIRTEEN	Into the Unknown	157
APPENDIX:	Clive Lloyd – Career Statistics	163
	Index	169

Illustrations

Clive Lloyd, with Walcott, Nurse, Sobers, Butcher and Gibbs
With Forbes Burnham, Prime Minister of Guyana
The Rest of the World XI, August 1970 SPORT AND GENERAL PRESS AGENCY
Clive Lloyd's century in Bombay, 1974–75
Lloyd the bowler KEN KELLY
Lloyd batting in contact lenses, 1972 ASSOCIATED SPORTS PHOTOGRAPHY
In the field, with Lance Gibbs PATRICK EAGAR
Batting in the World Cup Final, 1975 PATRICK EAGAR
Man of the Match for Lancashire, 1973
World Series Cricket victor, 1980 PATRICK EAGAR
First World Cup victory, 1975
Receiving the 1975 World Cup from the Duke of Edinburgh, 1975 PATRICK EAGAR
Lloyd's second Prudential World Cup trophy, 1979 KEN KELLY
Wedding day, September 1971
Clive and Waveney, with their two daughters

Hitting out against England
In full flow for Lancashire (three views) ASSOCIATED SPORTS PHOTOGRAPHY
With Ian Chappell in Australia, 1975–76

With Ian Botham, 1984
Greig c Lloyd b Daniel 116, Leeds 1976 KEN KELLY
Hitting John Snow for 4 PATRICK EAGAR
Aggressive batting v England
4 more for Lloyd KEN KELLY
A century v England at the Oval, 1980 PATRICK EAGAR
Sharing a joke with Dickie Bird ASSOCIATED SPORTS PHOTOGRAPHY

His 100th Test appearance, Kingston, Jamaica
Joel Garner, Michael Holding, Malcolm Marshall ASSOCIATED SPORTS PHOTOGRAPHY
Randall c Lloyd b Garner, Edgbaston, 1984 PATRICK EAGAR
Warming up at Lord's PATRICK EAGAR
A warning from Bird
Congratulations for Graeme Fowler
... and for Larry Gomes PATRICK EAGAR
With Dujon and Richards ASSOCIATED SPORTS PHOTOGRAPHY
'Blackwash' at the Oval PATRICK EAGAR
With Viv Richards
Harper, Garner, Lloyd, Richards at Lord's, 1984 PATRICK EAGAR
An honorary degree from Manchester University MANCHESTER EVENING NEWS
At the United Nations

Preface

Some months ago, I was sitting with Clive Lloyd in a discothèque in Bombay when a lady asked him to dance. The West Indian captain demurred and, pointing to me, suggested that she might possibly want to dance with 'my brother'.

On another occasion, when the West Indies were playing in a home series in the Caribbean, I was on my way to Alf Gover's indoor cricket school in south London, when a woman approached me and, in a state of some confusion, exclaimed: 'Mr Lloyd, I thought you were playing cricket in the West Indies. I never expected to meet you here. It's so nice to see you.'

Clive Lloyd has always been highly amused by the mistaken view of a number of people that we share some profound familial affinity. Greying rapidly and of infinitely smaller build, I've always been terribly flattered even to be mentioned in the same breath as so distinguished a man.

My admiration for Clive as a cricketer and for his undoubted success as captain of the West Indies stretches over many years, and comes as a feeble cry close to the acclamation of millions. And the wonderful thing about writing this book has been the eagerness of his friends and colleagues to assist.

It would be impossible to list the names of all those who did so, but the Lancashire 'crowd', Jackie Bond, David Lloyd and Jack Simmons, must take pride of place. Tom Graveney and the members of the current England and West Indies teams were more than happy to share with me their views of Lloyd the man, the player, the captain.

During the 1984 West Indies tour of England I had the good fortune to meet three Guyanese nationals, living in England, who indoctrinated me into the peculiarities which surrounded the development of early cricket in Guyana. I owe a great debt of gratitude to Sammy Devenish, Monty Walcott and Compton Glasgow. I trust I have done all my helpers credit.

I discovered very quickly that it would be impossible to write about Clive without the active assistance of his wife, Waveney. She is not only his greatest supporter but, much more than that, she is helper, critic, confidante, counsellor, mentor. Her generosity and warmth were as lavish as Clive's more extravagant strokeplay.

During the preparation of the manuscript I learnt of the death of Jock McCombe, an official of the Somerset Cricket Club, but more to the point an inveterate admirer and friend of West Indies cricket. He adored Clive Lloyd as he loved Viv Richards. I feel sure that after the West Indies success in 1984, which Jock never lived to see, when 'he passed over, all the trumpets sounded for him on the other side'.

I started to write a book about Clive Lloyd because I know him and like him as a man and as a player. Having immersed myself in research into his life and long career, and having talked at length to the extraordinary range of people who know him well, as well as to those with whom he has had only the briefest acquaintance, I became convinced that I was writing about one of the most phenomenal players of all time.

Neville Cardus had the wisdom to see in Learie Constantine a flair unique to West Indies cricket, and Constantine himself had a vision of what West Indies cricket, with time and application, could eventually achieve. Clive Lloyd was blessed with the perspicacity, the ability, the character and the opportunity to make Constantine's dream a reality.

To paraphrase Shakespeare's Brutus, Lloyd caught the tide in the affairs of West Indian cricket, took it at its flood and has led it to fortune.

Acknowledgements

It would not have been possible to write this book without a careful perusal of the considerable body of work which has already dealt with Clive Lloyd's career as a player and as captain, and with the unique nature of West Indian cricket. Nobody has written about the latter more brilliantly than the West Indian philosopher C. L. R. James. Equally important has been Tony Cozier's work on contemporary West Indian cricket; he is without question the authority on the subject, and although the book he wrote with Clive Lloyd (*Living for Cricket*) only went as far as 1979 it was an important guide to my efforts.

I am grateful to Henry Blofeld, Bob Willis and Sunil Gavaskar for allowing me to refer to their material, and to the England captain David Gower and the tireless David Frith for making me aware of comments they had recorded about Clive Lloyd.

Wisden played its usual role. No sport is blessed with a better book of reference, and the Secretary at Kennington Oval and his librarian kindly allowed me to 'take up residence' there for a considerable length of time.

Colin Cumberbatch, the Antiguan photographer, friend and keen follower of West Indies cricket teams around the world, never failed to return my enquiring calls, whether in London, Antigua or New York, and my ITN colleague and Sports Editor Mervyn Hall assisted in putting together the statistics of Lloyd's long career.

They all helped; errors of fact or perception are mine.

Once again, Rebekah Ponsford coped admirably with my disorderly working pattern and as typist was invaluable to the effort of producing this book.

This project would never have reached its completion without the expert, good-natured assistance of my editor Richard Johnson. His interest, encouragement and unfailing good humour saw me through.

CHAPTER ONE

Saluting the Captain

What we call the beginning is often the end,
And to make an end is to make a beginning.
The end is where we start from.

T. S. Eliot

It was about to come full circle.

In the glittering twilight of a brilliant career in international cricket, Clive Hubert Lloyd, who had dutifully served the West Indies Board during the most turbulent decade of its existence, and who as player and captain had quarrelled with it, resisted it and fought it on the most highly principled grounds, was about to be honoured by his masters.

The genesis of the Board's decision to honour Lloyd lay in a combination of the ineluctable forces of history and response to popular demand. Already the West Indies cricket authorities had been left behind by others. Clive Lloyd had been presented with the Order of Roraima, Guyana's second highest national award, to honour the fact that under his leadership the Guyana cricket team became the first in the Caribbean to win both major regional tournaments in 1983 (the Shell Shield, and the Geddes Grant and Harrison Line Trophy). At the Bourda ground a new stand had been named after him. The Trinidad Government had acknowledged his services to West Indies cricket by giving him the Chaconia Medal Class One: Gold, and in 1983 he had received honorary degrees from the Universities of Manchester and Hull.

At last, it was the turn of the West Indies Board. The setting was to be the fifth and final Test match against Australia at Sabina Park, Kingston, Jamaica, towards the end of April 1984. It was to be Clive Lloyd's 100th Test appearance for the West Indies. No other West Indian player had taken part in so many Test matches. In the days of fewer Tests the great Frank Worrell made 51 appearances. Lloyd's fellow-Guyanese Lance Gibbs and Rohan Kanhai each played 79 times for West Indies. Only Gary Sobers comes close to Lloyd's record with 93 Test matches, 85 of them consecutively.

In the politically charged cut-and-thrust of West Indian team selection, where cricket careers soar and plummet with such chastening speed and where for such a long time the consensus on team selection was only arrived at after the representatives of half a dozen islands had pressed the claim of their own national stars, survival for 100 Test matches, spanning 18 years, is no mean feat. Gary Sobers, who led the West Indies in 39 Tests, described in his book *Cricket Advance* the qualities needed if a West Indies captain was to survive: 'He has to be about half a dozen men, all rolled into one. He must have the nerve of a gambler, the poise of a financier, the human understanding of a psychologist, ten years more cricket knowledge than he can ever possess and the patience of a Saint.' Lloyd had shown all these qualities and he had survived.

But there was much more to Clive Lloyd's record than mere survival. Few captains in the history of cricket had been more successful. No West Indian captain had brought more honours to the region. In no other sport had West Indians been more successful and in no other sport had success mattered more.

This was Lloyd's record by the time he had led the West Indies to victory against Australia in the Jamaica Test: 100 Test matches, 161 Test innings, 18 centuries, and 6,904 runs at an average of 46.33. In the five years before his 100th Test match appearance, his average was over 70.

That fact caused Lloyd to observe recently that some cricket fans in the West Indies become too preoccupied with the advancing age of players! 'In England for example there've been fellows like wicket-keeper Bob Taylor, who was as agile and competent as anybody at the age of 42, and Geoff Boycott is still playing at the age of 44.' Against India in 1983 and against the Australians in the early part of 1984, Lloyd had proved conclusively that he was still among the best West Indian batsmen. In the Calcutta Test on the Indian tour his patient, controlled, responsible knock of 166, made in eight hours, had turned certain defeat into an epic West Indian victory, and in the third Test against the Australians in Barbados a few months later his score of 76 was as brilliant as anything scored by any other West Indian batsman in the match.

All that and more had been to Lloyd's credit. He had come to represent everything that was solid, durable, responsible and honourable about West Indian cricket. Not since Frank Worrell had any West Indian captain so forcefully stamped his influence on the team or on their game.

On countless occasions his contemporaries had argued with him. In the later stages of his long career, after he had become West Indies captain, he had frequently been the subject of bitter controversy. Fellow-players had taken issue with his beliefs about the way the game should be played and with his tactics on the cricket field. Some criticism of him had been continuous, even strident. But very few players failed to admire him and what he had done for West Indies cricket. And everyone found him fair, decent, generous and unfailingly magnanimous.

Something else added considerable distinction to Lloyd's success. The relationship between the West Indies Board and its players is not merely difficult, it is almost entirely confrontational. The confrontation arises because the relationship is predicated on the vastly different assumptions of both sides. The Board sees its duty as asserting its traditional authority on the governance of the game. The players, believing they have been stung for so long by the whiplash of both tradition and authority, tend to resent the Board, which claims to operate in their name. At various junctures in the history of the West Indies game, that simmering resentment has boiled over into open conflict.

Had that not been the case, Lloyd's 100th Test match appearance for the West Indies would have come before April 1984. And that year's series against Australia, in the West Indies, was a sharp reminder of what might have been.

Six years before, Australia's fourth visit to the Caribbean had been marred by bitter controversy, and Lloyd, who had by then led the West Indies in 29 successive Tests, winning 13 of them, had been at the centre of it all.

Like almost every other international cricket dispute of the period, the problem on that Australian tour was caused by the exodus of players following the inauguration of Kerry Packer's privately promoted World Series Cricket. In one very painful sense the West Indies Board had been dragged into the resulting chaos, very much against its will. The administrators of West Indies cricket are acutely aware of the special conditions in which the game thrives in the region. Partly because of that fact, when the first frantic round of international meetings were held in London to discuss how to react to Mr Packer's popular enterprise, West Indian cricket officials went out of their way to persuade their English, Australian and New Zealand counterparts to act with prudence and caution. The West Indians put it strongly to the other major cricketing nations that, instead of attempting to 'kill Packer off' (as one delegate incautiously put it), a course of action which was fraught with the most perilous legal implications, cricket authorities everywhere should rather face up to the legitimate challenge posed by the birth of a contemporary cricket idea – one with which the cream of the world's players had so quickly associated themselves.

But an agonised feeling of betrayal, a sense of outrage and deep hurt at Packer's audacity had been allowed to supersede the wisdom of the saner proponents of rationality. The authorities proceeded to take a series of decisions in the name of protecting the established game but in fact designed to punish those who had joined Packer's private promotion, to intimidate those who might be thinking of joining and to hound Packer and his revolutionary scheme out of the game. It had, in the end, amounted to one of cricket's less edifying spectacles. As Macaulay might have said, never had anything looked so ridiculous as the governing bodies of international cricket gripped in a fit of righteous indignation.

For a while, the West Indies prudently refused to allow themselves to be suborned into a course of witless spite. But in the end they responded to an impassioned call for a show of spurious unity. During the 1977–78 Australian tour of the West Indies, West Indian cricket administrators came face to face with the consequences of the actions of their counterparts in Australia, where the hatred of Kerry Packer was born and where disapproval of everything he stood for was as deep as the Church's inherent opposition to the satanic world of wilful sin.

Standing four-square on the principle of the sanctity of 'established' cricket, the Australian Cricket Board of Control had refused to select any of their Packer players for the tour of the West Indies. The result of that decision was obvious. The cream of Australia's cricket talent had been left at home. There was no Dennis Lillee, no Lenny Pascoe, no Greg Chappell, no David Hookes. All these were 'Packer' players.

In their place went one of the most inexperienced teams ever to leave Australian shores. To lead the young side the Australian administrators had persuaded the veteran former captain Bobby Simpson to go to the West Indies on tour. A few months earlier Simpson had been called out of retirement to lead a weak Australian side against India in Australia. Even so, he must have been surprised to be asked to take the team to the West Indies.

Sticking to their clearly enunciated and well-argued stand, the West Indies had maintained that they would only penalise their players if and when their commitments to Packer's World Series Cricket made them unavailable to play for their country, and not before. And since for the series against Australia at home all the West Indies players contracted to Packer were back in the Caribbean and ready to represent the West Indies, the banning option simply did not arise. The home team was once again to be led by Clive Lloyd.

It took no cricket genius to predict that the full might of the West Indies side, with its formidable pace attack and its dashing strokemakers, would be too much for the Australian band of innocents abroad. The first two Tests in Port of Spain and Bridgetown were won by convincing margins and well inside the allotted time. Going on to Georgetown for the third, Simpson's men were beginning to look like the remnants of Lord Cardigan's cavalry after the ill-fated Charge of the Light Brigade.

In islands where victory in Test cricket has long been equated with the far loftier themes of national progress and political independence, the West Indies cricket bosses could hardly feign displeasure at the success of their team. But nothing could adequately disguise the fact that the Australian team was second-rate. Nor could the West Indies administrators fail to be sensitive to the controversy which had resulted in the selection of such a weakened Australian side and the disproportionate strength of their own team.

Moreover, for the first time since Packer, the West Indies Board had been seen to be out of step with their Australian counterparts. Before the Australians arrived, the West Indies had been forced only into a restatement of principle. Now they had to live with the consequences of sticking to that principle. All this might have been tolerable had it not been for the fact that another factor, which had been building up in the minds of the members of the West Indies Board, now entered the equation.

Although, at those international crisis meetings in London in the wake of the birth of World Series Cricket, West Indian cricket administrators had defended the right of their players to make money wherever they could, there was deep disappointment, even downright resentment, at one significant aspect of the manner in which West Indian players had joined the Packer enterprise. Senior West Indian players had received Packer's emissaries, listened to the Australian's proposition, made up their minds and signed contracts all in the strictest secrecy demanded by Packer. To their new-found benefactor the players had demonstrated a loyalty which had conspicuously exceeded anything the West Indies cricket authorities could claim. In no single instance was this more dramatically illustrated than in the secrecy with which the West Indies wicket-keeper Deryck Murray joined the Kerry Packer group.

Deryck's father, Lance Murray, an affable and immensely likeable man, had been a prominent member of the Board. Deryck's uncle, 'Sonny' Murray, was an official of the Queen's Park Cricket Club, which runs the Queen's Park Oval in Port of Spain, the hub of international cricket activity in Trinidad and one of the most prominent grounds in the Caribbean. And Deryck Murray's employer at the Port of Spain headquarters of an international banking firm had been Jeffrey Stollmeyer, the President of the West Indies Cricket Board. Although all these people were so terribly close to what was going on under their noses, never in the weeks of the gestation of Packer's plans did a single word about the enterprise leak to any Trinidad cricket official or member of the West Indies Board. To their consternation and their chagrin, West Indian cricket administrators heard the news when the rest of the world did. If the Board was ever in doubt about the way it was perceived by the players, here was hard evidence indeed. In one lightning stroke Packer had secured the trust of players as the West Indies authorities never could. The West Indies Board was shocked. The total secrecy in which the Packer deals had been negotiated, the fact that not a single player had felt inclined to tip off the authorities, was considered a grievous wound.

So when, just before the first Test match in Port of Spain, the players presented their claims for better rates of pay for Test matches, the discussions quickly reached deadlock in an atmosphere rife with ill-feeling and recrimination.

With their earnings boosted considerably by the big money in World Series Cricket, there was little doubt that the West Indies players were not in the best mood for compromise. To this day Lloyd himself makes no secret of the fact that the money paid by Packer made the players aware for the first time just how much they were worth. So when they met the West Indies Board to discuss money, it was as though the Packer enterprise had given them the chance to air once and for all their long list of grievances against the West Indian authorities.

The most controversial move, though, was made by the Board. On the opening day of the series against Australia everything went decidedly sour when Deryck Murray, who had become the players' chief spokesman and negotiator, was abruptly relieved of the vice-captaincy. It was not unlike the kind of thing the West Indies Board had done before to the accompaniment of murmurs of protest, a few stinging newspaper editorials, but little else. This time, things turned out to be very different. Under Clive Lloyd and with a little encouragement from Packer, the West Indies players were far more confident. It was as though they had come of age. Together with Clive Lloyd, Deryck Murray had championed the West Indian players' case for better wages. The players saw the Board's decision to relieve Deryck Murray of the vice-captaincy as an act not dissimilar to the dismissal of a successful shop steward by a frustrated and spiteful company about to lose the opening round of bargaining to the workers.

After that, relations between the Board and the players plummeted to sub-zero. The inevitable occurred a couple of weeks later. Three young players, Austin, Croft and Haynes, put their names to World Series Cricket contracts, despite the fact that they had apparently given members of the Board verbal assurances that they would not do so. The Board, feeling friendless and beleaguered, decided that the time had come to punish what it saw as nothing short of treachery.

For their part, the players surmised that the Board was spoiling for a fight when it asked them to say long in advance whether they would be available for the West Indies engagement, a tour of India, later that same year. The Board had quite a legitimate point, arguing that the number of players committed to playing Packer cricket made it uncertain whether the full West Indies side would be available for the trip. The Board decided to omit from the side to play Australia in the third Test in Georgetown three players, Murray, Haynes and Austin. Their replacements were non-Packer players. It was not a brilliant stroke. To many it bore all the hallmarks of a desperate throw of the dice by a punter seeking to get even.

Even so, the Board might have succeeded had it not been for the courageous and principled stand taken by the West Indies captain, Clive Lloyd. He simply demanded that the Board should state very clearly 'the principles underlying the selection of the team' for the Georgetown Test. Perhaps the Board's longterm plans were clear, even sensible. But they could never in a million years have justified leaving out three seasoned players for a Test match against Australia.

Having made its stand, the Board could not afford to back down. It stood its ground. An impasse had been reached. Clive Lloyd resigned the West Indies cricket captaincy. In very few instances had the West Indies Board been so publicly challenged by any player.

There followed even worse news for the Board. The standing of the West Indies captain among his players was such that it took only a few hours for every other West Indian player contracted to Packer to follow suit and declare themselves unavailable for the third Test. It was a solidarity unlike anything the administrators of West Indian cricket had believed possible. They did not realise it then, but a discernible and significant shift in the balance of power had taken place between the Board and the players. From then on, for better or for worse, they were dealing with a captain who had a profound sense of the importance of West Indies cricket and of his role as a responsible guardian of its interests during his period at the helm. To the Board and to the West Indian public at large, Clive Lloyd had put down his marker. After that, nothing about West Indies cricket was to be the same.

Alvin Kallicharran, who had publicly dithered about whether or not he would join Packer's cricket competitions, was named West Indies captain, and a bemused team, with several new faces, flew to Guyana after one of the most earthshaking weeks in the history of the West Indies game.

There were threats from some cricket fans to disrupt the match in Guyana. These proved empty but there was little doubt that the rest of the Australian tour had been blighted by the controversy. The series ended in unseemly confusion with calls for the resignation of the West Indies Board and the selectors.

Neither Clive Lloyd nor his fellow West Indian Packer players felt responsible for the chaos. Lloyd argued strongly that he had taken on the Board over a matter of principle. He had broken no rules when he signed to play cricket for Packer in Australia. He and his fellow-professionals had returned home to play against Australia. The problem had been caused by the West Indian selectors. They had chosen to omit three players from the team for the third Test, although they had no real basis for that action – at any rate, not one that they could easily explain.

By taking the line he did, Lloyd confirmed that he was part of that new generation of West Indian players, confident of their ability and unafraid to pursue their legitimate interests, even if it meant confronting those who for decades had organised the game according to their own rules. Even more of a danger signal for the West Indies cricket authorities was the fact that the sympathy of the entire West Indian cricket-loving public went with Lloyd. Had the matter not been resolved, it would almost certainly have meant the decline and even death of West Indies cricket. But it was resolved, and it was not too long before Lloyd was back at the helm.

Now in April 1984, six years later, after an impressive record of international cricket success and during another Australian tour, the West Indies cricket authorities were about to acknowledge the services of a captain with whom they had not always seen eye to eye, but who had moulded the West Indies team into a formidable winning machine.

The occasion had been appropriately set up. The first two Tests against Australia were drawn. Lloyd suffered a recurrence of a nagging hamstring injury and had not played in the second. But he returned for the third Test match in Bridgetown, Barbados, to lead the West Indies to what seemed an improbable but proved to be a convincing victory.

The Australians had batted spiritedly to save the first two Tests and appeared certain to share the honours in the third when they scored 429 runs in their first innings. On a perfect batting strip the West Indies did even better. They replied with 509, Lloyd's contribution being 76, and the game seemed set for a high-scoring draw. But the Australians plunged headlong into disaster in their second turn at the crease. Only two Australian batsmen reached double figures as Malcolm Marshall and Michael Holding played havoc with the Australian reply. Marshall's analysis was 5 for 42, and Holding's four wickets for 24 runs in 15 overs ensured that Australia were given no chance to set the West Indies a decent second-innings target. Only 18 runs were needed for a West Indies victory and they were safely made by Greenidge and Haynes. So the West Indies had won the third Test by ten wickets.

The Australians fared no better in the fourth Test in St John's, Antigua. Batting first, only Alan Border with 98 and David Hookes who made 51 saved the tourists from total disaster as they were dismissed for 262. The West Indies' reply could not have been more confident. Before their home crowd, the Antiguan batsmen Ritchie Richardson and Viv Richards put on 308 runs for a record-breaking third-wicket partnership in the West Indies total of 498. Lloyd hit two sixes in his contribution of 38 before being caught at deep mid-wicket off the bowling of Rackemann. Facing the difficult proposition of scoring 236 runs to make the West Indies bat a second time, Australia's resistance again crumbled against the West Indies pace bowlers. This time the destroyers were Marshall and Joel Garner. 'Big Joel' bowled out half the Australian side for a mere 63 runs and Marshall took three wickets for 51 as Clive Lloyd's Caribbean cricket kings wrapped up the game with a full day to spare. Australia were swept away for a meagre 200 runs in their second innings. No player in Kim Hughes' team seemed capable of coping with the West Indies attack for long. The St John's wicket was clearly a good one, but that didn't help Australia. Their opening pair put on 50, but after Garner dismissed Ritchie for 23 and Phillips for 22 Australia never recovered.

It was the third Test ever played at the St John's recreation ground in Antigua and the first time a result had been achieved. The previous two – against England in 1981 and against India two years later – were both drawn.

Before his 100th Test match, the fifth and final in the 1984 series against Australia, Lloyd made a journey halfway round the world to appear in court in Sydney to defend what he called 'the honour and integrity of West Indian cricketers'. The matter arose out of an article written in the *Melbourne Age* newspaper in January 1982, under the headline 'Come On Dollar, Come On'. It referred to a one-day match between Australia and the West Indies, which the home side were required to win so that they and not Pakistan would meet the West Indies in the final series of matches in this triangular competition. The Australians won the game, but Lloyd's team, masters of the limited-over game, went on to take the final series by a convincing 3–1 margin.

To the West Indies, the article implied that they had been part of a set-up to ensure that the Australians, the bigger crowd-pulling team, and not the Pakistanis reached the finals. Lloyd told the court that the article suggested he had committed a fraud on the public for financial gain by pre-arranging with others the result of a qualifying match. He said he had been incensed by the article, which had threatened the West Indies standing in the world of cricket. The publishers of the *Melbourne Age*, through their lawyers, defended the action on the ground that Lloyd had not even been referred to in the article. (In fact Lloyd had been kept out of that particular qualifying game by injury.) But the West Indies cricket captain was awarded A$100,000 (£66,666) in damages for the article, which suggested that the one-day game had been rigged.

In every respect, then, the lead-up to Lloyd's centenary Test match could not have been better for the West Indies captain. Two-up against Australia at home with one Test to play. Batting first, the tourists' batting was again ravaged by the West Indies quick bowlers. Malcolm Marshall took 3 for 37, Joel Garner 3 for 42, and Australia were bundled out for 199. Gordon Greenidge, who made 127, and Desmond Haynes, who scored a patient 60, gave their team such a magnificent start that, although there was something of a crisis in the team's middle-order batting, the West Indies managed to take their reply to 305, a lead of 106. But even that was too much for Kim Hughes' shell-shocked side. The first three Australian wickets went cheaply and the tourists stumbled unconvincingly to a feeble second-innings total of 160. The West Indies openers knocked off the 54 runs required with no alarms, and the series had been won by Clive Lloyd's team by three matches to nil.

The skipper's moment of history had been acknowledged just before the final rites. The President of the West Indies Board, Allan Rae, made a warm speech and a presentation to Lloyd, and big Joel Garner spoke on behalf of the players. 'Clive Lloyd,' said the 'Big Bird', 'is like a father, big brother, guardian and guide to West Indian cricketers. We respect him because he respects himself and all of us. If Worrell led by inspiration and Sobers by example, Lloyd combines both to great effect.'

Long before Garner spoke, tributes to Lloyd were flooding in from every part of the Caribbean. Writing in a Jamaican Sunday newspaper, Michael Manley, that country's former Prime Minister, had this to say about Lloyd and about his leadership of the West Indies:

In Clive Lloyd, the captaincy found its figure of continuity. A great enough player to command unquestioning respect, Lloyd grew in stature, maturity and cricket judgement as the years passed. His reign is like that of some great monarch of the Renaissance . . .

To his virtues of leadership by example must be added the attributes of the man . . . the manner with his team is avuncular rather than authoritarian. He sets the example in personal discipline, in personal integrity, in personal performance, in personal dignity, in personal courtesy.

The former West Indies fast bowler Wes Hall, who knew Clive Lloyd in his early days as a fellow-player and who managed Lloyd's victorious team in India in 1983, wrote:

If, as Neville Cardus said, 'fame consists of being talked about by the largest number of perfect strangers', Clive Lloyd is a most befitting and shining example of it. He is admired by cricketers and chroniclers the world over, and he has dominated the panorama of international cricket for a decade, like a colossus.

Newspapers throughout the Caribbean emblazoned their sports pages with Lloyd's phenomenal record. As West Indies captain his record was especially impressive: 64 Test matches, 28 won, 11 lost, 25 drawn. He had won twelve of the series in which he led his team, and lost only two. And there were even greater deeds to come. Ahead of him lay a series against England in the summer of 1984, to be followed almost immediately by another battle down under with the Australians. Together they would mark the end of Lloyd's reign as West Indies captain. Singly or together they would indelibly stake his claim as one of the greatest sporting leaders of all time.

In geographical terms they were not very far away, but in every other regard Kingston, Jamaica, in April/May 1984 was a long long way from Georgetown, Guyana, in 1944, when Clive Hubert Lloyd was born.

CHAPTER TWO

The Beginning

> Demerara is the Elysium of the tropics – the West
> Indian happy valley of Rasselas – the one true and
> actual Utopia of the Caribbean seas – the Transatlantic
> Eden.
>
> Anthony Trollope

Despite Trollope's confident description of Guyana, or Demerara as it was commonly known in the nineteenth century, the perception of the country as part of the West Indies or the Caribbean owes much more to the idiosyncrasies of seventeenth-century European expansionism than to geography.

Guyana is physically part of the South American continent. Unlike the other Caribbean territories it is not an island. It does have the Atlantic Ocean to its north-east, but on its three other sides it is bounded by land. Surinam, the former Dutch possession, is due east. To the south sprawls the unending vastness of Brazil, and Venezuela is a frequently disputatious western neighbour. For a time the Dutch were the colonial masters in Guyana. The architecture of much of Georgetown, the capital, is still distinctly Dutch, and because the country was in the general vicinity around which the desperate search for the fabled city of gold, 'El Dorado', was centred, Spain maintained for long an interest in the region. But it was the British who stayed, and British Guyana, as it then became, was incorporated into the 'British Caribbean'. It made for administrative tidiness, if nothing else.

Politically, though, the country has always been somewhat ambivalent about its 'Caribbean' status. When in the late 1950s there was an attempt under Britain's sponsorship to link all the English-speaking West Indian colonies into a federation, Guyana took no part in the experiment. Then and later, with the exception of vital trade connections, the most durable link the other West Indian islands have retained with Guyana was forged by its participation in and its contribution to West Indies cricket. For Clive Lloyd, who was born in Georgetown on 31 August 1944, and for West Indies cricket, that has been a fact of singular good fortune.

The young Lloyd grew up in a Caribbean environment where

cricket was always much more than a game. In his book *The Middle Passage* the Trinidadian writer V. S. Naipaul explains:

In a society which demanded no skills and offered no rewards to merit, cricket was the only activity which permitted a man to grow to his full stature and to be measured against international standards. Alone on a field, beyond obscuring intrigue, the cricketer's true worth could be seen by all. His race, education, wealth did not matter. We had no scientists, engineers, explorers, soldiers or poets. The cricketer was our only hero figure. And that is why cricket is played in the West Indies with such panache.

The brilliant Trinidadian philosopher, C. L. R. James, puts it in even better perspective in his book, *Beyond a Boundary*. He says:

What do they know of cricket who only cricket know? West Indians crowding to Tests bring with them the whole past history and future hopes of the islands. English people for example have a conception of themselves from birth. Drake and the mighty Nelson, Shakespeare, Waterloo, the Charge of the Light Brigade, the few who did so much for so many, the success of parliamentary democracy, those and such as those constitute a national tradition. Undeveloped countries have to go back centuries to rebuild one. We of the West Indies have none at all, none that we know of. The sight of the three W's, Ram and Val wrecking English batting, help fill a huge gap in their consciousness and in their needs.

To James' penetrating observation should be added a remarkable fact. In all the political turmoil which preceded and resulted from the demise of the short-lived West Indian Federation, the only institution whose existence remained unchallenged was the West Indies cricket team. Indeed, in the agonising throes of the failure of the Federation, one fear haunted a largely indifferent West Indian population. This was the fear that the end of the political grouping would also mean the end of the West Indies cricket team. It was a lesson in the importance of cricket in the region that those senior West Indian politicians who saw the inevitability of the break-up of the Federation were the same ones who argued most strongly that the 'federal' West Indies cricket team should not be affected.

Clive Lloyd's father, who worked as chauffeur to a local doctor, was the West Indian exception which helps to prove the rule. He was *not*

mad about cricket. Nor did he dream of his son becoming another
Frank Worrell or Everton Weekes. But Clive's mother took an interest
in the game and cricket was in the family blood. The sister of Clive's
mother, a Mrs Gibbs, had a son some ten years older than Clive. His
name was Lance and he was destined to become one of the finest off-
spin bowlers in the world.

Lance lived close by; young Clive grew to know his cousin well and
despite the disparity in their ages they talked cricket endlessly. That
alone would have had a powerful influence on an impressionable
mind. But there was more. A few streets away from his family home,
there was a house which was always talked about in reverential tones.
It belonged to the West Indian batsman Robert Christiani.

Christiani had made his début against England in 1947, and had
also played for the West Indies against Australia, India and New
Zealand. No memorable cricket records stood to his name, but that
was of little consequence. To his proud compatriots one thing alone
mattered. He was Guyanese and he had represented the West Indies on
famous cricket fields abroad. That made him a local hero.

By the time Clive was a boy in his teens, Christiani's playing days
had come to an end, but he could still be heard doing radio commen-
taries, that staple diet of West Indian cricket fanatics. Other well-
known Guyanese cricketers lived close by. Colin Wiltshire and Colin
Hector played for one of the strongest teams in the country, the
Demerara Cricket Club, and the Lloyd family home was but a stone's
throw from the club ground.

Time which was not taken up aggressively playing cricket in
backyards, breaking glass panes in neighbours' windows or trying to
knock over the cardboard boxes which frequently served as wickets,
was spent watching cricket. Few of Clive's contemporaries even
contemplated buying tickets for big matches. Even if the disposition
had been there, money was always short. Only the élite paid their way
into the ground. The others, Clive included, watched their cricket
either by peering through spaces in the galvanised iron fencing which
closed off the ground, or from what Clive describes as 'the confines' of
prominent trees overlooking the ground.

Watching cricket this way in the West Indies is neither haphazard
nor unplanned. It is carefully thought out and executed with precision.
It has also bred its own expressions. Those intending to watch the
cricket from 'the confines' of nearby trees would never admit to not
having purchased tickets, but would say they had a 'bird ticket' – a
reference to those other occupants of the trees when no cricket is being

played. Ingenious 'bird ticket' holders even managed to wedge small stools or benches among the powerful branches of the larger trees, thus ensuring that they could follow the proceedings in some modicum of comfort.

Once in place, 'bird ticket' holders were understandably reluctant to desert their perches, even temporarily. So firmly did the habit take hold that a rudimentary pulley system would be devised to provide the day's food and drink. It worked with exemplary efficiency. Vendors would winch up drinks and sandwiches; money in payment would be sent on the basket's downward journey. At all times honour between vendor and buyer was exemplary.

'Bird ticket' holders at the Bourda ground provided a valuable ancillary service to fellow non-paying customers. The galvanised iron fencing around the ground was frequently breached by intrepid punters desperate enough to see the cricket to risk a blow on the head from a policeman's baton. From their vantage-point, the 'bird ticket' fans could assess the effectiveness of the security arrangements and inform their fellows which part of the fence it was safe to enter. This was part of Clive's introduction to the game.

Occasionally when the stars practised near the pavilion, eager young boys were allowed to form themselves into an army of fielders. They never had to be asked. Somehow what they did seemed automatic. They were simply drawn to the sound of bat on ball as moths are to an open flame.

The excitement of getting close to the players was indescribable. Young recruits were hardly ever allowed to bat, and only on the rarest occasions were they allowed to bowl. So fielding became a passion. And what a thrill it was to earn from a batsman the accolade: 'Great stop!'

Although their participation in these practice sessions was carefully circumscribed by unwritten rules of conduct, for a few treasured moments the young boys were able to rub shoulders with established players, stopping scorching off-drives, running after shots they had failed to stop and throwing the ball back to the bowlers with swelling boyish pride. Unlike some of his contemporaries, who were scornful of anything which did not hold out the promise of batting or bowling, Clive enjoyed fielding.

He had long legs and was quite a fast runner. At school he carried away many of the top athletic honours. By his early teens he had also developed a passing interest in body-building. It had all come about because a small tyre-repair shop, not far from where he lived, had in the course of its business collected a few rudimentary bits of weight-lifting equipment. From miles around the young boys congregated to test their strength and to improve their physique.

Running for his school and doing weight training in the afternoons after classes, young Clive Lloyd became something of a fitness fanatic. He played a little soccer, but cricket was his passion. It was the game to which he returned. By the time he was fourteen he was good enough to be made captain of his High School. His memory of the kind of captain he was at that tender age is blurred, but he does remember making several high scores and taking a number of wickets bowling his slow leg-spin. (He always batted left-handed and bowled right-armed.) And he was a keen fielder. His most important recollection, though, is of being allowed to play his cricket with complete freedom:

> I was pretty strong for my age [he says now] and I suppose I made as many high scores as any of my contemporaries, perhaps far more. Apparently whether I was hitting the ball handsomely over mid-wicket or over deep backward square, or driving hard along the ground, I was very correct. I remember one of our teachers, who was also President of the Umpires' Association, Rudolph Harper, would bowl off-breaks and leg-breaks to us, and I was always commended for striking the ball very well. So in fact nobody tried to change the way I played. Perhaps that was just as well. They wouldn't have succeeded anyway.

Clive was not yet fifteen when his father died in 1958. With the passing of the family breadwinner went all hopes of a young man's higher education. Clive was the oldest of six children – one brother and four sisters. His mother, an immensely resourceful lady, held her family together with that admirable determination and matriarchal skill so characteristic of West Indian mothers of the time. But life had changed for the entire family. Although a scholarship for further education was open to Clive, he was now obliged to forgo it in the interest of finding a job which would help supplement the meagre family income. This he did. He took a clerical job at the Georgetown hospital. It was, needless to say, poorly paid (£16 a month), but the routine nature of his duties had at least one clear advantage. It gave him the opportunity to concentrate on cricket – his first love.

Family connections and proximity to the ground dictated that he should join the Demerara Cricket Club's Division Two side. After only one game for the seconds he was invited to replace an injured player in the first team. So at the age of fifteen he made his first-team début at the famous Bourda cricket ground, an occasion he recalls:

It's really impossible to describe the incredible thrill it was to walk out onto the ground on which I had seen so many of my childhood heroes. But if you try to imagine what it was like: here I was, a young lad of fifteen, playing in the same match as those great names which had always been so famous to me. I think in that same match there were Norman Wight, Lennie Thomas, Colin Heron and George Camacho, all players who had represented Guyana with distinction. I suppose I felt just as a player, say, from a minor Cheshire league suddenly being called up to play for England at Lord's. It was just too much.

And perhaps it was. Clive Lloyd was out for 12 in his first big match at the Bourda ground, bowled 'through the gate'. He was clearly disappointed that he had never 'got in' (he was at the crease for less than half an hour), but he was thrilled just to have played. He also made a mental note that in future he must remember to get his bat closer to his pad in playing his shots. But he had not been unduly worried about his failure. It was therefore the cause of some distress to him to read only a few days later that the local sports press had virtually written off his chances of making it in the big time. He was particularly hurt to discover that the newspaper's view of his prospects as an international player had apparently been shared by none other than the great Robert Christiani. Christiani was to make an identical mistake a little later in Lloyd's career. It made such an impression on Lloyd that even today, some twenty-five years later, he is able to recall in minute detail the function at which the criticism was made and what he was eating at the time ('the starter was curried egg').

Such premature assessments about the ability of young players is not uncommon in the West Indies and is perhaps more a consequence of the surfeit of young hopefuls, who crowd senior competitive cricket every year, than a lack of perception or sheer bad judgement.

Clive Lloyd did not allow that kind of assessment of his talent to destroy his confidence. And he was lucky to have always had a small but devoted band of supporters. His biggest fan was the Demerara Cricket Club's captain, Fred Wills, a wonderfully big-hearted man who later became an outstanding lawyer and a minister in his country's government. He had personally helped Clive with his school work. Now he took a fatherly interest in his cricket. Knowing that money was scarce in the Lloyd household, Wills tried to encourage excellence at cricket by offers of financial reward. Clive describes what Wills would do:

> He would say to us before the start of a game: 'Anyone who gets a hundred today will get twenty dollars from me.' Then perhaps I would be out for 90, but after the match he would still give me the twenty dollars. And when on some other occasion I did score a hundred, instead of the twenty dollars he had promised he would increase the sum to forty. Fred Wills was a sensational man. He had a heart as big as a house, he knew what our problems were and he knew how to help.

By the time he was nineteen Clive Lloyd had become an established member of the Demerara Cricket Club, and even more pleasing to him and his supporters was the fact that he was always in the runs. It was hardly surprising, therefore, when he was invited to join in the series of trial matches for the eventual selection of British Guiana's national team to play in Barbados in 1963. But the invitation raised false hopes. He was left out of the first three trial matches and although he played in the fourth and final game it was virtually washed out by rain; he never faced a ball and failed to gain selection. He was bitterly disappointed. Older players, among them his cousin Lance Gibbs, a staunch advocate of Clive's cause, and the former Guyanese and West Indies bowler, Berkeley Gaskin, tried to console the young player, advising patience. He did not have to wait long. Later that season he made his first-class début against Jamaica in Georgetown and not a particularly distinguished one: he was caught at long-leg for 12.

In his heart Clive was all too aware that he was still terribly young, but he was desperately keen to do well. Forced by the death of his father to leave school at such an early age, he had abandoned all hopes of a career outside cricket. And having decided on cricket, he simply wanted to get on with it. But there were more disappointments to come.

When the Australians toured the West Indies in 1965, Lloyd was named emergency fieldsman in the Guyana Test and actually ran onto the ground once to carry a message from the manager, Frank Worrell, to the West Indies captain, Gary Sobers. But that was as far as his aspirations to full international cricket went that year. And indeed in the following season they seemed to plunge even further when, playing against a star-studded Barbadian side which was led by Gary Sobers and included Charlie Griffith, Seymour Nurse, Robin Bynoe and Conrad Hunte, Lloyd was dismissed for a 'duck'. He had been fooled by the Sobers 'chinaman' and was trapped leg-before. It was his first face-to-face encounter with the complete mastery of the great Sobers, and Lloyd never forgot it.

Guyana had made a first-innings total of 227, Butcher falling only one short of his century and Kanhai playing a typically brilliant innings of 69. But the real terror of Guyana's innings had been Garfield Sobers. Bowling fast-medium and slow left-arm, he took six wickets for 56 runs and broke the back of Guyana's batting. In that first innings Lloyd never got a look in.

When Barbados batted the hero of the piece was again their captain and inspiration, G. Sobers. His contribution this time was a memorable double century out of his team's 559 for 9 declared. Facing a deficit on first innings of well over 300, Guyana's task batting a second time was formidable. With Sobers and Charlie Griffith in full cry, runs were difficult to come by. But Lloyd fought with great patience and determination and kept his head while everyone around him was losing theirs. His 107 was his team's top score, but with support coming only from Joe Solomon, who stayed with Clive for a long time to make 70, and Kanhai, who made 43, Barbados won the match comfortably by an innings and 15 runs. It had been a victory set up and then sealed by Sobers.

Four days later, on 26 February 1966, Clive Lloyd took the field for his country against Jamaica at Sabina Park, Kingston. Jamaica were bowled out for a modest score of 222, and Guyana and Lloyd took their chance to go well ahead on first innings. This time Lloyd's contribution was an almost flawless 194 out of a score of 421 for 9 declared. It was the innings around which the impressive total had been built. The only batsman to come close was the redoubtable Rohan Kanhai, and he had only made 61.

The Jamaicans pulled themselves together when they batted a second time and made amends for their miserable first-innings score by making 404 for 9 declared. Thus the match ended in a draw. But Lloyd had good reason to be pleased with his showing. His teammates proudly predicted that his big score against Jamaica would be the first of many.

It was a confident Lloyd, therefore, who travelled with the Guyanese party to St Kitts two days later to play against the Windward and Leeward Islands. He batted once and scored only 40, but he had been striking the ball well and had already begun to distinguish himself in the covers as a fieldsman of the highest quality. With long loping strides he swooped on shots played to the offside and with what seemed an unbroken action he would turn and hurl the ball right over the top of the stumps into the wicket-keeper's gloves. Guyana beat the Windward and Leewards easily by six wickets and Lloyd went back to Georgetown to await the selection of the West Indies team to tour England.

A few days later the composition of the touring party was announced, but the name C. H. Lloyd was not included. The fact that he failed to make the England tour of 1966 was almost certainly a direct result of the manner in which West Indies teams of the time were selected. If the process resembled anything, it was far more like the striking of a political bargain in a smoke-filled room in the American Deep South than a calm and reasoned assessment of the cricket talent available to the selectors. Not even the notorious Mayor Daley of Chicago did more horse-trading than the representatives of the various West Indian islands on the selection committee. In their favour, it has to be said that each island's representative was subjected to enormous pressure by the press and the cricket public well before he sat down with the other selectors to choose a touring party. And selectors who failed to force their countrymen into West Indies teams were roundly condemned in the media and later made scapegoats for any failures of the team. Selecting West Indies has always been a thankless occupation.

What the young Clive had no way of knowing was that his omission was almost entirely 'political'. Each island had stood out for the inclusion of certain players in the squad. To 'buy' support for its players, an island representative would agree to back the 'choice' of some other island's selector. Somewhere in the horse-trading, Guyana had slipped up. In the big trade-off the Guyanese representative on the selection committee had failed to give his support to a Barbados player and the Barbados representative responded by refusing to support Lloyd's claim for a place in the touring party. None of this had anything to do with cricket.

Years after he had ceased to be West Indies captain, Gary Sobers, who had seen and applauded Lloyd's century against Barbados only days before the team for England was chosen, was to comment that Lloyd's omission for the 1966 touring party had been one of the graver errors made by the West Indies Board.

But in 1966 Clive Lloyd, just after his 21st birthday, knew nothing of these dire machinations. He was shattered by his exclusion and to this day becomes quietly silent and introspective when remembering how hurt he felt. Uppermost in his mind were the consequences of failing to make it. In a society where the fine cricketer is thought of as a hero, the converse is equally true. The inability of a cricketer to succeed is regarded as such an unmitigated disaster that it has been frequently used in West Indian drama as a metaphor for the darkest tragedy.

The 1966 West Indies touring party might not have had the approval of all Guyanese, but it performed with great credit. Sobers, Nurse, Butcher, Kanhai, Holford, Hunte, Lashley, Hall, Griffith, McMorris, Gibbs, Allan and Hendricks proved more than a match for Cowdrey's England side. Of the five Test matches played, the West Indies won three, England one, and one was drawn. The man of the series was Sobers. He scored 161 in the Manchester Test, was not out 163 at Lord's, and made 174 at Headingley. In the Leeds Test he shared in a record fifth-wicket partnership of 265 with Seymour Nurse, and at Lord's he put on 274 for the sixth wicket with his cousin David Holford. It had undoubtedly been Sobers' tour. To Clive Lloyd, listening to the progress of the West Indies on the radio at home in Georgetown, all this was poor consolation.

The injustice which kept him out of that victorious West Indies side ended a few months later. For the party to tour India towards the end of 1966 and in the early part of 1967 included the name of C. H. Lloyd.

Even now [says Lloyd] I can remember as if it were yesterday my exhilaration at being selected to tour with the West Indies team. I was beginning to learn what an incredible leveller cricket is. A few months before I was so distraught at not being chosen to play against England, now all that was behind me and the prospect of India beckoned. I learnt such a great deal. The country, of course, was fascinating. Some 50 per cent of Guyanese came originally from India. So it was interesting to see the origins of so many of my countrymen. Travelling about over such long distances to play various fixtures made one realise what a vast country India is. We all got warnings about how careful we should be about the food and water in some parts of the country and a few of our players suffered a little, but I was lucky.

On the cricket field Lloyd learnt a lot too.

It was [he says] my first prolonged encounter with Indian spinners.

Some of the wickets were quite slow, but there was invariably a lot of bounce and the Indian wrist-spinners made the ball bounce and turn. I tried to play them by using my height, going down the wicket and killing the spin. Of course I was merciless on anything short and also learnt to sweep the spinners to leg.

At the outset, I realised that although I had been included in the touring party, getting a place in the Test side would not be very easy. The West Indies middle order was not a bad one ... Kanhai, Butcher, Nurse and Sobers. But just about the luckiest break in my career was the fact that Frank Worrell happened to be in India on some kind of lecture tour and he was kind enough to have quite a few chats with me. For example, he indicated that he felt that I had been unfairly left out of the previous team to tour England. But he quite sensibly pointed out that I might have gone and not done terribly well in conditions in which I had not played before. That might have affected my confidence. So he said that I should put that completely out of my mind and concentrate on getting among the runs on wickets which were more like those in the West Indies. It was sound advice.

But getting into the star-studded West Indies team was still the problem – especially since the young Guyanese had not exactly distinguished himself in the minor games in the run-up to the first Test in Bombay. With a top score of 39 his form had not been outstanding.

The first Test against India began in Bombay on 13 December. Lloyd had been unaware that Nurse, the stylish and heavy-scoring Barbadian, was uncertain whether he could take the field because of a nagging injury. So his surprise was total when, an hour or so before the toss, Sobers told him that he was in the side. A great chapter in West Indies cricket was about to begin.

How do you describe your feelings at achieving all that you have ever wanted in life [Clive says now]? I tried to contain my happiness but it was not very easy. Luckily it was mixed with considerable nervousness and I was terribly grateful when the Indian captain, Pataudi, won the toss and elected to bat first. That meant that I could at least work off some of my nervousness on the field before having to perform with the bat.

India's innings began inauspiciously. They were three down for 14 before a fourth-wicket stand between the Indian captain, Pataudi, and

Durani put on 93 valuable runs. They played Hall, Griffith and Sobers with admirable skill. India's real saviour, though, was Borde, whose contribution of 121 helped his team to semi-respectability and a first-innings tally of 296.

The West Indies reply began somewhat patchily. Hunte batted with a wonderful mixture of defensive skill and aggression. But his partner Bynoe was out for two, Kanhai fell for 24, Butcher for a mere 16, and although Hunte was progressing smoothly towards yet another Test century a sound West Indies stand was important. Lloyd had been given just about the ideal opportunity to prove himself, and he was ready to take it.

The big danger was clearly the Indian spinner, Chandrasekhar. An attack of polio had left Chandra with a slight impediment in his right arm and had given him what Lloyd describes as a 'freakish action'. The result was that the ball came off the pitch quickly, much faster than from conventional spinners; it bounced a great deal and frequently turned sharply too. There had been a lot of talk in the dressing-room about Chandra but very little useful advice about how he might be played. All three West Indian wickets had fallen to the Indian wizard.

Almost immediately Lloyd had a stroke of singular good fortune. Deceived by Chandra's faster ball, he fenced outside the off-stump and was put down at slip. Gradually he began to work out a pattern to deal with the scourge of the West Indian batsmen. Instead of waiting on the back foot and then trying to decide which way the ball would turn, Lloyd decided to play off the front foot.

He says:

I felt that with that policy, playing on the front foot, I could do two things. I could reach out and smother the spin, and I could also minimise the danger posed by those deliveries which tended to skid off the pitch. So I decided to play Chandra purely as a googly bowler. Because his leg-break didn't turn a great deal, I was fairly safe on the front foot. The other thing in our favour was the fact that India depended almost entirely on their spinners. And although with other bowlers like Durani and Venkataraghavan it was top-class spin all the way, their attack lacked, I feel, variety. What that meant for me was that once you found your rhythm there was really nothing in the bowling to disturb that.

After his let-off in the slips, not a great deal disturbed Lloyd's rhythm in his maiden Test match. He played forward to Chandra, watched the other bowlers carefully, and anything straying down the legside was swept off the middle of the bat for four. His partnership with Hunte blossomed and their fourth-wicket stand realised 110 runs before Lloyd was caught at the wicket off Chandra for 82. By then, though, the West Indies were well on the way to a good first-innings lead. A rapid half-century by the West Indies captain and a truculent 80 by David Holford made sure of that. Hunte had made his hundred, but there was little doubt that the first day's honours had been stolen by Lloyd. 125 runs adrift after both teams had batted once, India managed 316 when they batted a second time. But that left the West Indians with only 192 runs to get to win the match; four wickets went down, but Lloyd was there at the end.

However, victory was not achieved without some panic. Lloyd recalls:

> The wicket began to wear a little and on that kind of a surface the Indian bowlers could be sheer hell to play. Three West Indian wickets fell cheaply and a fourth fell before we had got to a hundred, so there was a little panic. The only guy who didn't seem to believe there was even a vague possibility that we might lose the match was Gary. He and I came together after Hunte was out and he calmly instructed me to play carefully until Chandra and the other Indian spinners got tired and strayed off line, after which, he said, we could get the runs quickly so that he could listen to the races on the radio. He said he'd been given a 'hot tip'. I could hardly believe my ears. Here was I playing in my first Test match and the captain was apparently more concerned about winning at the races than winning the Test. But he was right. The Indian spinners did seem to get a little tired, we were able to accelerate our scoring and in the end we won the match with time to spare.

At the moment of victory Lloyd was left undefeated with 78. After his 82 in the first innings, it had been a memorable introduction to Test cricket.

The West Indies won the second Test mainly because they were lucky enough to have the best use of a bad wicket, and having gone two-up in the series and feeling that there was hardly any need for further exertions they almost lost the third. But Sobers stepped in near the end to ensure that the game was saved and the West Indies went home undefeated.

The Indian tour had also been a success for Lloyd. He had scored

760 runs in first-class matches on the tour; he had made his maiden century in West Indian colours against a Prime Minister's XI in Delhi; he had scored 138 against Ceylon, and he was second only to the great man Gary Sobers himself in the overall first-class batting averages. To be well ahead in the averages of players of the reputation of Butcher, Hunte, Kanhai and Nurse was to achieve far more than he believed possible on his first overseas tour.

More important for the future of West Indies cricket, though, and for his own career as West Indies captain nearly ten years later, Lloyd began to observe some of the darker and less professional sides of West Indian cricket. His determination to change these when he became captain accounts to a great degree for the enormous success of the West Indies under Lloyd. Some of these are worth noting briefly.

Lloyd found that the team which went to India lacked discipline. There had been very little team consultation about how to cope with the opposition. Players, and senior players at that, responded boorishly to Indian hospitality and Indian interest in them. And by and large the Indian team had been beaten because the West Indies had had the better side. It was not because of the application or professionalism of the West Indian party. It had been a party of individuals led by a brilliant skipper. There was nothing cohesive about the unit, there had been no *esprit de corps*. If he were ever to be given the responsibility of leading a West Indian side, Lloyd later thought, the job must be discharged according to a different and higher standard.

The West Indies won two of the three Tests on that Indian tour and took the series, but they found it impossible to hide the fact that Sobers' team was one in transition. Hall and Griffith were playing out their last days in international cricket. Gibbs and Sobers had bowled well, but new players were needed to spearhead the West Indies attack.

Clive Lloyd was destined to have an important voice in the shape that the West Indies attack of the future would take.

CHAPTER THREE

How the Captaincy Evolved

All experience is an arch wherethro' gleams that untravelled world . . .

Tennyson

This Lloyd is going to be a power to come in the West Indies batting when he matures.

Brian Close

The character of Lloyd's leadership of the West Indies team was shaped by the idiosyncratic pattern into which the story of contemporary West Indian cricket fitted. And thus its formation began long before he assumed the captaincy of the West Indies side, in some ways long before he became a player. Thoughts of his own evolved later, but in a deeply significant sense were a synthesis of all that had gone on before.

A convenient point of departure is 1950, generally acknowledged as the birth of modern West Indian cricket. Of that period, none other than the great Learie Constantine has written: 'I have always held the view that until 1950 the West Indies rarely played cricket of which they were capable.'

Since Constantine had himself ceased playing by then it was a particularly generous view, but the evidence for his conclusion is strong enough. In 1950 the West Indies beat England for the first time in a series. The significant aspect of their victory was that it had occurred in England.

Two years earlier, England, believing that the West Indies were a pushover, had sent a weakened team on tour to the Caribbean. It was most unsuccessful, losing the last two of the four Test matches played. But in the view of many commentators the West Indian victory had not counted for much, having been achieved against an MCC side from which many of the better England players had been missing. In nothing more was this reflected than in the fact that the man chosen to lead the MCC, Gubby Allen, was 45 years of age. There was no Compton, Edrich, Washbrook, Alec Bedser or Yardley. The West Indies duly won at Bourda by seven wickets and, three weeks later, beat England by ten wickets.

Two years later in England, Ramadhin and Valentine wrecked a bemused England team with their baffling and unreadable spin and ushered in a new age of West Indian cricket. The two players, unknown at the start of the tour, took 59 Test wickets between them and were immortalised in calypso for helping their side to a victory by 326 runs at Lord's.

Neither the England team nor English cricket writers could quite believe what was happening, and some commentators formed the view that the West Indian victory at Lord's was a flash in the pan. In a particularly ungracious comment *The Times* of London was moved to observe before the Oval Test match that 'the West Indies would sink into a slumber of insolent security'.

But the West Indies batsmen proved wide awake and pugnaciously secure. Worrell led the way with a stylish 138, Rae scored 109 and the West Indies posted a first-innings total of 503. Only the great Len Hutton with a magnificent double century had any answer to the West Indies' attack, and England were made to follow on. This time, Valentine took six wickets for 39 runs, England were bundled out for a miserly 103, and the West Indies crushed England by an innings and 56 runs.

The sounds of the impromptu celebration calypsos which were first heard at Lord's and which reverberated around a crowded Oval ground at the end of the series, sent an echo of pure joy far across the Atlantic to the Caribbean. Ramadhin and Valentine, 'those two little pals of mine' as the calypsos called them, and the three W's, Worrell, Weekes and Walcott, had put a new face of success on West Indies cricket by defeating England at home by three Test matches to one.

It is not always appreciated that the West Indies victory in 1950 could not have come at a more politically significant time in Caribbean terms. A few years before, West Indian patriots had begun the drive for political self-determination in the colonies. The first studies on the feasibility of West Indian self-government had just been published. In Grenada and Barbados, in Trinidad and Jamaica, talk of political progress for the islands filled the air. It was the spirit of the times.

A few years later it was to lead to an irreversible loosening of the control of the West Indies colonies by the metropolitan power and the attempt at a broad-based, self-administering West Indies Federation. The fact that the Federation was destined to fail is not terribly relevant here. The die had been cast. Times had changed. The ineluctable flow was towards political independence from Britain. Never again would it be possible to put back the clock.

This was the climate in which West Indian politicians were seeking some kind of international justification to bolster their case for a greater say in the way their islands were run. They found it in the success of the West Indies cricket team in England in 1950. This is no exaggeration. Addressing a mass political meeting in Port of Spain, in what his party had called 'the university of Woodford Square', Eric Williams, just before he became the first Prime Minister of an independent Trinidad and Tobago, drew heavily on the West Indies success on cricket fields in England to make his case for political independence of the 'mother country'. 'In 1950,' he said one evening, 'we went to learn. Now we go to teach. The West Indies have arrived. We are no longer second-class.' In the words of C. L. R. James: 'The intimate connection between cricket and West Indian social and political life was established so that all except the wilfully perverse could see.'

Having provided a suitable metaphor for the commencement of the drive to West Indian political self-determination, West Indian cricket failed to keep pace with the changing times. Nothing illustrates this better than the return visit to England by the West Indies in 1957. Two years earlier, the West Indies had played hosts to Australia. Although the West Indian team of the time had been virtually built around the feats of Worrell, Weekes and Walcott, the West Indies Cricket Board decided in its wisdom to make Denis Atkinson, a white Barbadian insurance salesman and comparatively inexperienced Test player, Jeffrey Stollmeyer's vice-captain. It had been such an incredible decision that the view was formed very strongly that it was simply an attempt by the West Indian cricket authorities to make sure that the West Indies team was always led by a white man. Many years before, Learie Constantine had related with dignified scorn how the rumour had spread among the islands that it was the wish of the West Indies players themselves that they be captained always by a white man and that many had said that they would never play under a black captain.

Atkinson's appointment against Australia, though, was a bomb-shell, and when Stollmeyer missed three of the five Test matches through injury the inexperienced and totally unsuited Atkinson found himself leading a team in which there were far better players and far better captains than he was ever destined to be. To complicate matters, Atkinson was not only asked to lead the team but also to ignore, while attempting to do so, vociferous calls that he be sent back to sell insurance in Bridgetown. It would have been a test of character even for a much better player. Atkinson, it must be said, was not a personal failure during the series. In the Barbados Test match he scored a double century and took five Australian wickets, but he was never capable of leading the West Indies team and should never have even been considered for the task ahead of the more illustrious names in the team. Despite the consistent batting of Walcott and Weekes, the Australians won the first Test by nine wickets, the third by eight wickets and the fifth at Sabina Park, in Kingston, Jamaica, by an innings and 82 runs. Clyde Walcott distinguished himself by getting a century in both innings of that ill-fated Test match, 155 in the first and 110 in the second, but coming in response to Australia's massive first-innings total of 758 (Harvey 204, Archer 128, McDonald 127, Benaud 121 and Miller 109) the West Indies suffered one of the most crushing defeats they have ever endured against a visiting side.

It would be naive to imagine that players like Walcott were unaware at the time of the extraordinary policy of the West Indies Board towards the appointment of West Indian captains. Writing after his playing days were over, Walcott makes it clear that the 'Atkinson affair' was spotted in its making, long before the Australians arrived in the West Indies. In his book *Island Cricketers*, Walcott writes:

Before the Australians arrived in the West Indies the Board did something which at first seemed strange in announcing the names of the captain and vice-captain for our tour of New Zealand which was to take place almost a year later. The names were Denis Atkinson and Bruce Pairaudeau. Only after this announcement had sunk in, and had caused a good deal of controversy, did the Board announce that Jeff Stollmeyer and Denis Atkinson would be captain and vice-captain respectively for the Australian series about to start. Although it was hard to see why the announcement of the officials for New Zealand had to be made so far in advance, the apparent discrepancy in selection was more easily explained.

West Indies had no delusions, nor false politeness about the strength of New Zealand cricket and they had decided to send a young side, omitting all but a few of our established Test players. The choice of Atkinson as captain and – to gain experience – as vice-captain against Australia was in line with this policy. The public were not slow to ask why the 'three W's' had been left out of the reckoning, particularly after Frank Worrell had been vice-captain against MCC during the 1953–54 series. The public feeling seemed to be that the West Indies Board did not relish the prospect of having a coloured captain . . .

Shortly before the first Test Jeff Stollmeyer hurt a finger in practice so had to withdraw from the side. Automatically, his vice-captain, Denis Atkinson, succeeded him, but the press and the public took this as an excellent opportunity to renew their plea that Worrell should be given the captaincy. They rightly made the point that he was the more experienced player and captain, but they overlooked the fact that the thing had been decided in the selection room some time before and was unlikely to be changed now.

Atkinson's experience was, in fact, very slight. Until his selection to captain the side to visit New Zealand he had not normally led his colony, Barbados. But after the announcement, John Goddard, the usual Barbados captain, handed over to Atkinson, presumably to help the younger man gain experience. And so, lacking experience and the full confidence of West Indies cricket followers, Denis had a difficult task which was not eased when he had the misfortune to lose the toss . . .

It should be said that Clyde Walcott firmly stated his belief at the time that one of the reasons for the curious conduct of the West Indies Board probably had something to do with their reluctance to appoint a professional captain, a precedent which, he pointed out, 'despite Len Hutton's reign as captain, still has its roots deeply laid in England'. But only a few years later his guard slipped and his usual generosity vanished when he predicted that the white Barbadian player, Robin Bynoe, would only have to make 'fifty in one innings and he'll be captain'.

Suffice it to say that by 1957, when the West Indies team went to England, their first visit after their great triumph seven years before, dissension and internal wrangling had bitten deeply into the body corporate of their side. John Goddard, who had stepped aside from the leadership of the Barbados team to give Denis Atkinson the required experience, was brought back to captain the West Indies at the age of 38. It is true that by 1957 the England batsmen had worked out a method of neutralising the spin of Ramadhin and Valentine. Their rule had been a simple one. If you cannot read what the bowler is doing, play him off the front foot as an offspinner, thrusting the pad forward as a second line of defence if the ball still beats the bat. At Edgbaston, May and Cowdrey used the tactic effectively. Never in danger of being adjudged leg-before, since the ball was making contact with the pad such a long way from the stumps, they padded merrily on as the West Indian spinners grew hoarse with their unavailing appeals. The episode almost finished Ramadhin, but Frank Worrell was later to observe that the West Indian performance had been terrible: 'The kind of fight we put up was shabby.' The first Test at Edgbaston ended in a draw, but England won the second at Lord's by an innings and 36 runs, the fourth at Headingley by an innings and five runs, and the fifth and final at the Oval by an innings and 237 runs.

It was the appointment of the light-skinned Gerry Alexander as West Indies captain in succession to John Goddard that precipitated the powerful movement within the West Indies to have a black man as captain. Alexander had led the West Indies to victory against Pakistan at home in 1957–58 by the convincing margin of three Tests to one and had been chosen to take the West Indies to India. None of the three W's was available for the tour. The West Indies beat India easily, but one incident lingered in the minds of black West Indians and fuelled the perception that there was some Machiavellian plan by the authorities to ensure that Frank Worrell never led the West Indies as fulltime captain. On the Indian trip the Jamaican quick bowler, Roy Gilchrist, had been sent home by his captain apparently after a disagreement over the bowling of beamers. Gilchrist was a wiry young man with a fiery temper. He had been brought up in rural Jamaica. He might have found it difficult to accept the decisions of any captain, but many people writing at the time saw the affair as a clash between 'black plebeian Gilchrist and the light-skinned Cambridge graduate, Alexander'.

A campaign was started to have Gilchrist reinstated into the West Indies cricket fold, but the Board, without ever stating precisely how the dispute between Gilchrist and his captain had arisen, steadfastly refused to change its mind on the question.

C. L. R. James wrote of the episode:

The Board simply could not understand its responsibility for Gilchrist. It thought it could just excommunicate him and adopt the pharisaical attitude that we were no longer responsible for what he did. They were terribly – and may well be catastrophically – wrong. Gilchrist, we were reliably informed, was bowling bumpers and beamers at league batsmen, an altogether reprehensible and, what was more, dangerous business. He was a West Indian Test cricketer. Unless the Board discovered a way of scrubbing him white, he would be considered one of us, whatever decrees the Board might issue.

While the Gilchrist affair made headline news in the West Indies,

Frank Worrell, who had been completing his university studies in England, was expressing the view – through interviews on the BBC's Overseas Service – that Gilchrist should be 'helped' back into the game. That too was ignored by the authorities. Ill-feeling about the whole affair continued to build up and became linked with the issue of the captaincy and leadership of the West Indies side. Quite simply, the view began forming that, had Worrell been the West Indies captain, Gilchrist would never have been banished from the team.

Little attention was paid to the gathering storm of protest about the whole way West Indies cricket was run – until it burst into the open during the second Test match against England in Port of Spain in 1959–60, several months after Roy Gilchrist had been sent home from India.

On the first two days of the Test England, helped mainly by Barrington, M. J. K. Smith and Dexter, were all out for 382. Saturday, the third day, is always a big one for cricket in the West Indies and the Queen's Park Oval was brimming over with a crowd of some 30,000. Everyone hoped to see a spirited West Indies response to England's respectable first-innings total. The home side began at 22 for no wicket and were very soon in all kinds of trouble. Trueman, in particular, bowled brilliantly. With the help of Statham he cut a swathe of destruction through the West Indian batting, which left the usually noisy and ebullient Trinidadian crowd silent in its incomprehension and its disappointment.

The top half and the middle order of the West Indies batting accounted for, the England bowlers relentlessly pursued the tail-enders. With the score at 98, and seven West Indian batsmen already back in the pavilion, the young Trinidadian spin bowler, Charan Singh, was run out. He had not made many runs, nor could it possibly have been thought that he would by some miracle transform the outlook of the game for his side. And although the run-out decision was close, few felt that Singh had been the victim of an umpiring mistake. But from all parts of the ground bottles and stones began to pour onto the field. The missiles were not aimed at the English players. Indeed some were thrown in the direction of the pavilion. The Prime Minister of Trinidad, Dr Eric Williams, in the company of one of his ministers, Learie Constantine, went onto the field to try to appeal for calm. But play for the day had to be abandoned. Riot police were summoned to put an end to the disturbance.

The incident, over which the Prime Minister of Trinidad immediately dispatched a cable of apology to the MCC, had very little to do

with the fact that the West Indies were about to be crushed by England
in a Test match in Port of Spain. The much more likely explanation is
that the outburst was the climax of years of frustration at the peculiar
and at times self-serving manoeuvrings of the West Indies Board.
Almost immediately after the bottle-throwing incident at the Queen's
Park Oval, a Trinidad party political paper launched the campaign to
get rid of Gerry Alexander as captain and to replace him with Frank
Worrell. The paper had from its inception championed the case for
political self-determination for the islands of the West Indies. Now it
was in the vanguard of the battle for self-respect in West Indies cricket.
The writer was C. L. R. James:

> I had been waiting to get a sight of Alexander as captain and before
> the Test was over I launched an attack against his captaincy;
> Alexander must go. I based it on Worrell's superior experience and
> status and Alexander's errors of judgement. I refused to make it a
> question of race, though I made it clear that if the rejection of
> Worrell was continued I would reluctantly have to raise the racial
> issue. To have raised it would have switched the discussion away
> from cricket and involved all sorts of other issues. The anti-
> nationalists, with their usual brazenness, would have countered
> with 'Race introduced into sport'. And in any case everybody in the
> West Indies understood what I was leaving out even better than
> what I was actually writing.
>
> The effect was beyond all expectation. The *Nation* was an official
> organ and a highly political paper . . . This was politics and very
> serious politics. The 'Alexander Must Go' issue was sold out by the
> day following publication. People who had read or heard of the
> article rushed around looking for copies to buy. The man in the
> street expressed deep feelings: 'Thank God for the *Nation*.'
> 'Someone to speak for us at last.'

The James campaign was a long one. He repeatedly invited the
authorities to reply in justification of their actions, but the invitation
was never seriously taken up. Perhaps it was because the West Indian
cricket authorities really had little or nothing to say. Their actions,
well intentioned though they might have been, were thoroughly
indefensible.

In his foreword to Jeffrey Stollmeyer's book *Everything Under the
Sun*, E. W. Swanton, the doyen of cricket writers, made this comment
about the change from 'white leadership':

Looking back it seems even more evident now than it did at the time that Stollmeyer should have been the bridge between the white leadership of the early days and that which was available from the middle fifties in the shape of the exceptionally gifted Frank Worrell. In extenuation of the regime, it should be mentioned that Worrell was twice offered the West Indies captaincy before he was able to accept it.

Those offers were inconsequential to thinking West Indians. Worrell was being offered the job of leading the West Indies against teams like India. The West Indian patriotic campaign, so closely allied to the political climate of the time, had been to get Worrell chosen as captain against England or Australia. Few could claim not to see the difference.

Many years before the James campaign to dump Alexander and make Worrell West Indies captain, Keith Miller wrote in his book *Cricket from the Grandstand*:

> Another problem in the West Indies is that the captain has usually been chosen from among the European stock. Just think of the most famous West Indies cricketers ... Learie Constantine, George Headley, Frank Worrell, Everton Weekes, Clyde Walcott ... are all coloured, but none has led his country.

C. L. R. James, the *Nation*, and a following of hundreds of thousands of people throughout the West Indies changed all that. Frank Worrell became captain of the West Indies team to tour Australia in 1960–61, and in the clinching pointer to the relationship between cricket and politics in the West Indies, the Prime Minister of Trinidad and Tobago, Dr Eric Williams, had this to say in his address to the Fourth National Convention of his party, the People's National Movement (PNM), which owned and operated the *Nation*:

> If C. L. R. James took it upon himself to wage a campaign for Worrell as captain of the West Indies, and in so doing to give expression not only to the needs of the game, but also to the sentiments of the people, we know as well as he that it is the *Nation* and the PNM to whom the people will give praise.

In that statement lay an expression of the ultimate fusion of political interests and the game of cricket. The same paper which had strongly argued the case for West Indian self-government also argued the case for a black West Indies captain.

The rest is history. Worrell took the West Indies to Australia and although the West Indies lost the series, a hundred thousand people crowded the Melbourne streets to say farewell to Worrell's side.

Inheriting the West Indies captaincy at the age of 36, Worrell was a pragmatist above all else. Before he could think of shaping a winning side, he was forced to set his sights on the seemingly more modest but equally significant job of making a team out of a faction-ridden bunch of players, who had found some decisions of their governing body contemptible and who had bickered endlessly among themselves. Stopping that was Worrell's first job.

Thus when he arrived in Perth in 1960, in charge of the team for the first time, he said quite openly that winning the series against Australia was not his main aim. He had come to play attractive cricket. He was calling on his team to achieve at least something of which they were known to be capable. All the while, he would try to shape a team. His valedictory 1963 tour of England ended with the words:

> I have had a great run and as I have satisfied my greatest ambition in the last two years . . . I have no complaints. My aim was to see the West Indies moulded from a rabble of brilliant island individuals into a real team and I have done it.

Many years later Clive Lloyd was to have that same quiet but fierce pride in his ability to coax a collection of 'island individuals' into a fiercely competitive side. By the time he became captain he could take the process further and try to put together a winning side. But that was only possible because Frank Worrell made the start. He had been history's man for the job. He had with quiet satisfaction fulfilled what had been required of him. After that, it was up to his successors.

The man who followed Worrell was the greatest of all modern cricketers, Gary Sobers. Sobers was no great captain, no reader of his men as Frank Worrell had been, but rather an instinctive cricketer of stunning ability who provided a kind of leadership by example, but who would insouciantly gamble with the fortunes of his team and with the pride of West Indies cricket. He did it most grievously in the Port of Spain match of the 1967–68 MCC tour of the West Indies. He did it in a manner which made a deep impression on Clive Lloyd and helped shape his view about the seriousness with which Test cricket should be played. Lloyd was only beginning his Test career in that series against

England, and any thought of captaining the West Indies could not have been further away. In his first Test he had come up against Sobers' passion for horseracing, but he had never thought that Sobers could be so reckless with the result of a Test match at stake.

The point should be made at the outset that throughout the series against England, Sobers, as batsman, three bowlers rolled into one, and superb close-to-the-wicket fielder, performed magnificently. He scored 545 runs, including 113 not out in the second Test match in Barbados and 152 and 95 not out as his team vainly tried to level the series in the final Test in Guyana. And he accounted for 13 wickets in the series. But he it was who made it necessary for the West Indies to try to share the honours for the tour in that final Test match, by his declaration in the Test before – a declaration which that eminent recorder of West Indies cricket and well-known cricket commentator, Tony Cozier, has described as 'one of the most disputed in the game's history'.

The West Indies had effectively put the game beyond England's reach with a first-innings score of 526 for 7 declared. Solid performances from the young Guyanese batsman, Steve Camacho, who had come into the side as a replacement for Conrad Hunte, and centuries from Seymour Nurse and Rohan Kanhai, had made that score possible. Together Nurse and Kanhai had put on 273 runs for the third wicket, Nurse getting 136 and Kanhai 153.

Cowdrey's masterly 148 and the batting of Alan Knott, playing in his first Test series, shored up the England middle order, and even when Basil Butcher became the unlikely hero of the West Indies attack, taking five wickets for 34 runs, the match seemed as good as dead. England had avoided the follow-on. The West Indies led by 112 in the first innings and when they went in again only six hours were left, the wicket was playing well and there was no hint of rain. The West Indies batted without any urgency until 35 minutes after lunch, when to the surprise of the two batsmen in the middle and to the consternation of the crowd, Sobers got out of his chair and called his players in, thereby declaring the innings closed. The score at that time had been 92 for 2. Sobers left England to chase 215 runs to win the match, in 165 minutes.

What seemed incredible at the time, and remains so to this day, is the fact that there was no fast bowler on the field to be used either as part of a shock attack against the surprised England batsmen or to be used to slow down the over-rate and reduce the flow of runs when the target was getting nearer. Griffith had been sitting in the pavilion for most of the match with a leg injury. So Sobers took the new ball himself, with the offspinner Lance Gibbs in support. Had it not been for the venue, the crowd might well have been comforted in the belief that they were watching high comedy or some cruel theatrical farce. England unsurprisingly reached their target with three-quarters of their batting intact and with more than an over to spare. Sobers had to be given police protection when he left the ground that night, and his effigy was hanged and burnt in downtown Port of Spain. His attempt at explaining away his reckless declaration cut no ice. He said that he had been upset by England's negative tactics during the game and was determined to bring at least one Test match in the series to a conclusion.

High-sounding though those sentiments might be, they amounted to nonsense. Sobers had acted with total disregard for professionalism. When the day began the West Indies were 6 for no wicket. At lunch, two full hours later, they were 72 for 1 – 66 runs in 120 minutes, hardly the rate of a side batting with a declaration in view.

Some English commentators, grateful beyond measure for Sobers' gift of a Test match, found it easy to forgive the West Indies captain, arguing that had he won the match he would have been fêted by the entire Caribbean. But that was fanciful talk. The fact is there was never the slightest possible chance of that. It was left to Brian Close, the former England captain writing at the time, to make the withering observation: 'No captain declares to give the other side a chance to win. He declares only to suit his own purposes.'

Clive Lloyd, who was in the West Indies dressing-room at the time, agrees:

> I remember that terribly well. It didn't make any sense then and it makes even less now. We were all quite mystified about what Sobie was up to. The point about it all for me was the way it happened. There had never been any consultation among the senior players. I doubt Sobers talked to anyone about his declaration. That's why we have so many team meetings and team discussions in the modern professional game. Everyone knows what's required of him, but there's also an allround appreciation of what the team as a whole is trying to achieve and how. That kind of Sobers' declaration could never happen again.

Lloyd had been taught a profound lesson. Although the buck stops with the captain, cricket is and must always remain a team game. The process of bringing the players into the general decision-making, not on the field but beforehand at team discussions, was to be the guiding principle of his captaincy.

But all that was for later. For now, his main concern was holding his place in a star-studded West Indies side and attempting to fulfil the early promise which he had shown. He had certainly begun well enough. He scored 118 in the first Test against England at the Queen's Park Oval in Port of Spain, and got another century in the third Test match in Barbados. In that game his partnership with Butcher moved Brian Close to write:

The policy was still the same. Attack everything in sight, and how magnificently Lloyd and Butcher did it. Their first 50 came in 56 minutes, the next in 29 minutes and only greed for more runs brought their partnership to an end. Butcher, looking for a second run with the ball near the boundary . . . was run out. The rest . . . belonged to Lloyd as he strode gloriously to his second Test century of the series in only 157 minutes. He was fortunate but any batsman must be fortunate to survive in an innings of this kind as Lloyd treated every delivery bowled to him as a potential four. He edged one delivery from Brown between Cowdrey and Graveney in the slips. He swung at Pocock and might have been caught by Cowdrey. He looked out caught behind early on in the innings when he hooked at Snow. Parks and Edrich fielding at backward short-leg appealed confidently, but Umpire Jordan remained unimpressed. Thereafter no bowler was safe against Lloyd as he reached his 100 in 157 minutes with fourteen fours, one five and a six. Then he celebrated with the biggest six of the match, lifting Pocock over the schoolchildren's stand into the adjoining car park. This Lloyd is going to be a power to come in the West Indies batting when he matures. At the moment his enthusiasm overtakes him. He often plays the ball too far away from his body and on many occasions has no idea where the ball has gone when he has connected. But his century was as marvellously exciting as it was spectacular with the West Indies caning the England attack for 284 runs from only 53 overs.

CHAPTER FOUR
Learning in Australia – and Elsewhere

> Even though they [the West Indies] were winning
> consistently, they were still an unpredictable side who
> had retained the sense of adventure and fun which
> they show playing cricket at a far lower level . . . in
> Barbados or Berbice . . . In a way they are like impul-
> sive gamblers who begin to lose and go on doubling
> and redoubling their stakes regardless.
>
> Henry Blofeld

The West Indies tour of Australia in 1968–69 confirmed Clive Lloyd
as a player of immense potential but at the same time showed up what
has frequently been described as the vastly unpredictable nature of
West Indies cricket. The team under Sobers walked away with all the
honours in the first Test at Brisbane, beating Australia convincingly by
125 runs. And then, incredibly and almost without good reason, the
West Indies were hammered by the Australians in three of the
remaining four Test matches. For Clive Lloyd there had never been a
better or sadder demonstration of how cricket teams should not be led.

Lloyd is very kindly about Sobers' approach to the captaincy,
although his own methods were to be far different. And he puts the
blame for the Australian débâcle squarely on the absence of direction
and the lack of discipline in the West Indies team.

The problems began with the team selection. Lloyd says:

It was just another example of the selectors not doing their job
properly. It was quite incredible really, but the majority of our
players were on the wrong side of thirty and not even the kindest
person would say that they were fit. That was one of the first things I
discovered to my surprise when I joined the team, there was no real
emphasis on keeping fit. Of course, the other problem was that the
older players were no longer good enough for a strenuous and
difficult tour. It was unfair to Hall and Griffith that they were again
asked to spearhead our attack. Their playing days at this level had
slipped by. They were over the hill and yet they were selected. On
the other hand, Deryck Murray, only 27 at the time, was left out.
Now, what kind of policy was that? What building for the future

was being done? The main questions, of course, were being asked about the way Sobers handled the side. That's probably right, because the captain must take the blame when things fall apart, but I think he was badly served by the selectors and by the choice of the manager. I must say I thought Berkeley Gaskin, a man who had done a great deal for cricket in the past, was now a very much older person, in his sixties at the time I think, and quite frankly he was unable to take any of the pressure off the skipper. Sobers felt very much that professional cricketers were 'big men', capable of looking after themselves. Well, that's OK if the players do look after themselves, but when they don't a strong hand is needed. There was no one to give that on that Australian tour. Could you believe there were no training schedules, no really hard, organised practice sessions and no team meetings to discuss how we should approach the game? It was quite unbelievable really. Things have certainly come a long way since that time. The game we play now might not be all that different, but our approach is different.

The first Test at Brisbane gave no hint of the agony the West Indies were to suffer. Kanhai and Carew were the main contributors to the West Indies first-innings score of 296. Centuries by Ian Chappell and Bill Lawry helped the Australians to within twelve runs of the West Indian total, and in his team's second innings Lloyd got among the runs.

It came just at the right time really. I had been having a little bit of a struggle to get runs and didn't quite know what was wrong and what I should do. Things seemed no better when I was out for 7 in the first innings. I didn't begin too well in the second innings; perhaps it was just the fact that I so desperately wanted to settle in and play a long innings. But gradually I began to middle the ball and began picking up a few runs, which was just as well because we were in a little bit of trouble then. I think we were something like 170-odd for 6, when Joey Carew and I came together. I think one point which seemed to work in our favour was the fact that Australia's mystery spinner, Gleeson, who flicked the ball out of his fingers and confused batsmen about which way it would turn, didn't like bowling to left-handers. It's strange that Chandrasekhar didn't like bowling to left-handed batsmen either. And Joey and I were both left-handers. So that helped us and gradually I began to gain confidence.

Lloyd did much more than that. He and Carew helped to rescue the West Indies from a terrible position, and he himself went on to score a marvellous century. He was finally out when he was trapped leg-before by the Australian pace bowler, Graham McKenzie, using the second new ball, but by then he had scored 129. He hit 18 fours and one towering six, almost out of the ground, but what really appealed to the Australian crowd was the exciting way in which his innings developed. One hundred of his runs came in the final session of play. The next day the Australian papers were full of admiration for Lloyd's rescue act: 'Big Clive slams Australia', 'Lloyd's century to the rescue' and 'Lloyd puts Windies on top'. Many commentators noted the uninhibited way Lloyd played once he had found his touch and marked him out as the West Indies batting star of the future.

When Australia batted a second time, a tremendous bowling performance by Sobers, who took six wickets for 73 runs, tore the heart out of their batting and left them a long way behind the West Indies.

It had been a more than satisfactory performance by the team and by Lloyd. Adding considerably to his pleasure of getting among the runs after a lean spell was the fact that, to the consternation of the Australians, he had also taken two valuable wickets in Australia's first innings.

This was, I suppose, an example of Gary's genius on the cricket field. Lawry and Chappell had got on top of the West Indies bowling and everything had been tried to dislodge them but nothing seemed to work. They had both scored hundreds when Sobie tossed the ball to me. In those days I bowled rather gentle off-breaks and I don't know, maybe the Australians thought there were a few easy runs to be made here off the non-recognised bowler, Clive Lloyd. They looked at a few, and then having satisfied themselves there was no malice, they decided to have a go. Lawry was caught at midwicket trying to hit me out of the ground and Chappell was caught at cover. To rub the batsmen's noses in it a little bit, Gary himself took both catches. And as quickly and as surprisingly as he brought me on, he took me off.

That was the only time the West Indies played well during the tour.

We went from bad to worse [says Lloyd]. It was incredible. I missed the second Test through injury. My Christmas spent in bed was made more painful by hearing on the radio how we were being thrashed by Lawry's side. We lost the second Test at Melbourne and we were comprehensively beaten in the third at Sydney. I had recovered by then and got 50 in the first innings, but somehow it didn't seem to matter, you got the feeling things weren't going well. I got 40-odd in the Adelaide Test which we managed to save. That was a great morale-booster, but in the final Test we were set over 730 runs to chase and lost by 382. Lawry played the game as hard as anyone I have ever known and we just were not up to much. We were ill-equipped and we were exposed. The hardest part was to think after Australia that we still had to play five weeks more cricket in New Zealand. Not surprisingly, we didn't do well in New Zealand and had to return home having shared a series with what was considered the weakest team on the Test circuit.

Clive Lloyd's personal performances during the Australian/New Zealand series were not bad, but everything had been overshadowed by the team's abysmal showing. In 19 first-class matches and 33 innings he had scored 1,292 runs for an average of just over 41. But he had only really come good in the first Test match in Brisbane. On the New Zealand leg of the tour his batting in the Tests never reached the heights of accomplishment he had set himself. In one free-scoring match against South Island he hit a double century, but he would gladly have traded that for a few respectable scores in any of the three Tests. The West Indies won the first in Auckland, but then were beaten in the second by six wickets. The third and final Test failed to produce a result.

Back in the West Indies, the big postmortem about the loss of the Frank Worrell Trophy to the Australians began. The assessment was emotional, but not unrealistic. One Barbadian writer put the matter succinctly. Commenting on the team the West Indies had taken to Australia and New Zealand, Don Norville of the Barbados *Advocate News* said: 'The time has come for some tree-shaking to let the old fruit drop.'

Wisden searched for a deeper cause of the West Indies failure, although it did agree that some of the West Indian players were past it:

Age had taken its toll and the West Indies were victims of their own temperament, for when things began to go wrong they weren't able to regroup mentally and take a cool look at their problems. Sobers, their captain, with his ability might have been able to do that, but he seemed unsure of what was happening.

Assessing the failure of the West Indians in Australia, Henry Blofeld, the English cricket writer and commentator, had this to say in his book *Cricket in Three Moods*:

In Australia they [the West Indies] were the weaker of the two sides, but in losing as badly as they did ... they were like impulsive gamblers, who go on doubling and redoubling their stakes regardless. In each of the last four Tests, when things were going from bad to worse for them, their batsmen, including the older and more experienced, got out playing even more outrageous shots the worse the situation became. Their temperaments would not allow them to buckle down and slowly to fight their way back onto an even keel. It is no more their way of cricket than it is their way of life. When things are going well for them this approach is fine, but when it was going badly it made the side appear to be at times almost a laughing-stock. There were some specific cricket reasons to explain why they were beaten as they were, but they all really fit under this general heading. The captaincy fell some way short of the standard set by Worrell ... As a cricketer, Sobers is supreme and would have been supreme in any age, but as a captain the sharp instinct, on which his game is based, leaves him ... As a player, Sobers has never known serious failure. His amazing talents have enabled him to overcome every obstacle he has faced. He has never had to work out the game for himself in the way of all other cricketers and this has meant he is unaware of many of cricket's problems.

Lloyd's view of the failure of the side which went to Australia in 1968–69 has much more to do with the cricket played by the team and much less with the oft-repeated criticisms of the so-called West Indian temperament. He says:

We lost because we played badly. We dropped so many catches that it would have been a travesty had we got away with that kind of performance. Dropping catches has nothing to do with temperament. And the team as a whole was unfit, badly chosen and not equipped. People are always quick to jump to conclusions about the temperament of West Indies cricketers when we lose. But it all has to do with the way you play the game. If you play professionally, you win; if you don't, you lose.

But the whole Australian/New Zealand tour was to prove very useful for me in the future. I learnt several things. I learnt that a captain must lead or he certainly must try to. He must also be able to inspire his players. And I learnt most of all that there must be the freest discussion of problems within the team. Everything on a player's mind must be able to be aired at team meetings. We must work out what we are about. Everyone must be clear about that so when we take the field no one is in the slightest doubt about what is required of him and what is the team goal. Sobers failed in that. It wasn't the age of team discussions or team strategies. I was amazed at one get-together of players to hear one manager suggest that we should bowl full tosses at one Indian batsman, who would be so surprised that he might hole out at midwicket or something. That's no way to run a team meeting. That's not professional cricket.

One great era of West Indies cricket had come to an end. Clive Lloyd was destined to have a significant role in the shaping of the next. And he felt that the experience he gained as a member of the West Indies team which was so badly beaten by Australia in 1968–69 would prove invaluable.

But that was not to be for some time yet. By the late spring of 1969 the West Indies were off again, this time for a short tour of England.

One small incident even before a ball was bowled in the series showed the disarray and the lack of professionalism which were quite common at every level of West Indian cricket. The West Indies team had been chosen in the West Indies at a meeting on Sunday, 9 March. But the selectors had deliberated without the benefit of the captain's report on the previous Australia/New Zealand tour. It could, of course, be argued that what went on out there had been well-documented in the press and clearly visible in the poor showing made by the West Indies, but the fact that his report was not considered annoyed Gary Sobers. He felt that, as West Indies captain, what he had to say merited some attention. The point, though, was that there was no Sobers report to be found before the meeting. Sobers insisted that he had posted his report 'express' on Monday, 3 March. Six days later it had apparently not arrived. As a result, the West Indies captain expressed his disapproval that the party to tour England had been chosen before his report could be considered. What a way to run a railroad! No wonder, then, that it was not the happiest of West Indies tours.

Ray Illingworth took over as England captain since Cowdrey was unfit after an Achilles tendon operation, and Hall and Griffith, those veterans of West Indian triumphs in the early 1960s, had been left behind. Nurse, thoroughly disenchanted after the Australian débâcle a few months before, had announced his retirement from Test cricket, and Rohan Kanhai was unavailable because of injury.

England won the first Test at Old Trafford easily. Their first-innings total of 413 had been diligently compiled with a patient century from Boycott and half-hundreds from Edrich, Graveney and D'Oliveira. The West Indies reply was a lacklustre score of 147 in the first innings, and although they batted slightly better the second time around to make 275, their batting in the face of some accurate and hostile pace bowling from Snow and Brown was simply not good enough. The England victory was achieved by a margin of ten wickets.

The second Test match was a much more evenly contested affair. A century opening partnership between Fredericks and Camacho was followed by a workmanlike hundred by the young Trinidadian batsman, Charlie Davis, playing in only his fourth Test match. Chasing the West Indian first-innings total of 380, England began badly but recovered to get within 36 runs of their target. The main contributors to the England reply were Hampshire, who scored 107, and Illingworth, who recorded his first Test hundred in his 32 Test matches.

When the West Indies batted a second time, Lloyd played a brilliantly fluent knock for 70 in just over an hour and a half, for once restraining his tendency to hook at anything pitched short but driving beautifully off the back foot and pulling through midwicket with memorable ferocity. The West Indies declared at 295 for 9, and England were given five hours to make 332 runs, a challenge which fell by the wayside when Boycott took two and a half hours to make fifty. Wickets fell, but not quickly enough for the West Indies, and England were 295 for 7 when stumps were drawn on the final day.

The final Test match at Headingley was an agonisingly close affair. England scored a modest 223 in the first innings, but reduced the West Indies to 161 in reply. Sobers' five wickets for 42 runs when England batted a second time kept their score in check and they only managed to get 240. The West Indies in their second turn at the crease got the highest total of the match – 272 – but fell short of the England aggregate by 30 runs. The final session had been a thoroughly frustrating one for the West Indies. They seemed to be going well with Butcher in splendid form, but when he was caught behind off Underwood, a decision which might well have gone his way, four West

Indian wickets fell for only nine runs, and England snatched victory.

If the West Indies were lining up a long list of Test match defeats to their name, Clive Lloyd's patchy form did not help. He says:

It was not my best tour. To begin with, I think the weather at the start of the series didn't help us very much. It was wet and cold and some of our players were quite new to this.

I was having problems with my technique. I had always got a lot of runs playing the hook shot, but now it just didn't seem to be working. Instead of hooking the ball down, I was hooking it in the air which meant that unless it cleared the field, you're out caught in the deep or something like that. The only innings of consequence for me was the 70 in the Lord's Test match, but batting in the position I did – number six – players are supposed to get the odd hundred now and then to keep their place and to be of service to their side. Clyde Walcott, the team manager, and I had a chat about my hook shot and he advised me to resist the temptation for a while. It didn't cure the problem but I felt a little better for having had some advice, a chance to talk about things. That was much more than could be said in the general team sense. We were still not a thoroughgoing professional outfit. Discipline was badly lacking. There was a kind of division between the older players and the younger ones. The older ones seemed to be able to opt out of the matches they didn't feel like playing in and nobody encouraged the younger ones or helped them with any problems. There were very few discussions about how to approach matches. It was deplorable really. There was nothing that you could call team spirit. Everyone behaved very much as they wanted really and you cannot win Test matches against England in England with that kind of approach. As a matter of fact, I'd be surprised if you could win Test matches anywhere behaving like that. But we were really in the doldrums then. Nothing seemed to go right. In the Headingley Test match, with the ball seaming so much, we should have done much better, but we didn't. The good old days were well and truly over and no serious thought had been given to building for the future. I had struggled so hard to get into the West Indies side and to keep my place, but I was getting pretty fed up with the manner in which the whole business had been run. It's not very often that you can't wait for a tour to end. I couldn't wait to see the end of the last Test match.

Again, Lloyd had made runs outside of the Tests, but he had failed when runs mattered most. At Swansea against Glamorgan he got a fine double century, hitting the ball to every part of the ground and lifting many shots out of it altogether, and at Taunton he made 128 against Somerset. But the fact that he was second only to Basil Butcher in the team's batting averages gave him little comfort. On the tour he scored 904 runs, for an average in all first-class fixtures of 56.50.

CHAPTER FIVE

Frustration

There was no doubt about it, we were about to go into
the doldrums and it was one of the most disheartening
phases of my entire career.

C. H. Lloyd

Clive Lloyd had no thoughts of playing professional cricket in England
when, on his first tour of India, Wes Hall talked to him about a club in
the Lancashire League for which George Headley had played in the
1930s and which had taken on J. K. Holt, the Jamaican opening
batsman, and Clairmonte De Peiza, the Barbadian wicket-keeper
batsman, in more recent years. The name of the club was Haslingden,
and they had a place for an interested overseas player. Lloyd did not
have to give the matter a great deal of thought. He was embarking on a
career in cricket and he was being given the opportunity to earn money
for playing the game as a professional.

So, after the Indian tour, stopping only briefly in the West Indies, he
headed for Lancashire and Haslingden. Lloyd was happy to play
professional cricket and Haslingden were pleased to have a Test player
on their books. He worked hard at his batting, realising that the club's
investment in him must be seen to pay. He also knew that to a great
extent he was the club's big attraction and was determined not to let
the fans down. Very soon his big hits out of the comparatively small
club ground became the talk of the surrounding area, and it was hardly
surprising that word spread to Manchester and Old Trafford, less than
twenty miles away.

During the 1967 season Lloyd had the additional advantage of
playing for Derrick Robbins' XI, and his performances for that side
caught the eye of officials at Old Trafford. Back in the West Indies for
the 1967–68 tour by England, he eventually received an offer from
Lancashire. He returned to England in the summer of 1968 to play his
last season for Haslingden and to qualify for his new county side. That
year he easily topped the batting averages for the League club, scoring
over 1200 runs at an average of 56.

The 1970s did not begin inauspiciously for Clive Lloyd. In his first
full season for Lancashire in 1970, the club won both the John Player
League and the Gillette Cup and finished third in the county cham-

pionship. Lloyd's most enduring memory of that season was a great century against Kent at Dartford.

I got 163 [he says]. The thing I remember most about it was the fact that before the match, unknown to me, Derek Underwood boasted that he had a plan not only to restrict my scoring shots, but to get me out. He confided this bit of information to the Kent West Indian player John Shepherd. Anyway, I was in great form on that day, and I hit seven sixes in my score of 163, most of them out of the ground. And apparently, as I was told later, every time the ball soared out of the ground off Underwood's bowling, Shepherd would go up to Underwood and say: 'Is that the special ball you had for Clive, Derek?' I had great fun. My 163 was scored almost in even time and after that there was no stopping me for the rest of the season.

And then after that, there were five Tests for the Rest of the World against England, which had come about because of the cancellation of the South African tour of England. It was an honour to be in a team with such great names – Eddie Barlow, Barry Richards, Rohan Kanhai, Mike Procter, Mushtaq Mohammed, Intikhab Alam, Lance Gibbs, Farouk Engineer, Deryck Murray and with Gary [Sobers] as captain. I batted well. I got 400 runs, including centuries at Trent Bridge and Edgbaston, and was looking forward greatly to playing the Indians in the West Indies.

The five Test matches for the Rest of the World against England confirmed in Clive Lloyd's mind that he had reached the top of his profession. To distinguish himself in such élite company was one of the more pleasurable experiences of his career. But it was all to go badly wrong against India.

If in playing against England (and winning) the West Indies seek a kind of justification, an expression, a visible demonstration of political development and sophistication to match that of the former metropolitan power, different instincts make Test matches against the Indians a matter of the fiercest national pride. Those instincts are deeper in origin and more primeval than the desire to defeat the old 'mother country'. Part of the reason for this lies in the fact that, when India play in the West Indies, they find a great deal of support for their efforts among the substantial Indian population, particularly in Trinidad and Guyana. This never fails to niggle Afro West Indians, and that annoyance is in itself a reflection of the sometimes uneasy

Above The big time at last: Clive Lloyd (back row, right, next to Basil Butcher and – in the centre – his cousin, Lance Gibbs) with (front row, left) Clyde Walcott and Garfield Sobers.

Below With one of his greatest fans, the Prime Minister of Guyana, Forbes Burnham.

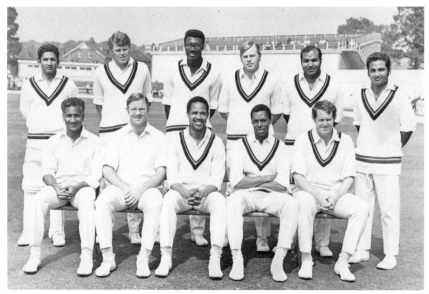

Above The Rest of the World XI, August 1970. Back row, left to right: Deryck Murray, Barrie Richards, Lloyd, Procter, Intikhab Alam, Mushtaq Mohammad. Front row: Kanhai, Barlow, Sobers, Gibbs, Graeme Pollock.

Below Congratulations from an Indian spectator in Bombay on a fine century by Clive Lloyd in the 1974–75 series.

Right Lloyd was a useful stock bowler before cartilage operations restricted his movements.

Below For a while he wore contact lenses. Here he is batting in the Benson and Hedges quarter-final, between Lancashire and Leicestershire in June 1972.

On his way to a match-winning century
in the World Cup Final against Australia
in 1975.

Right Clive Lloyd was a brilliant
outfielder and, later, a fine slip fielder.
He has always had a safe pair of hands –
although here his cousin, Lance Gibbs,
makes sure.

Award-winning time. *Above left* Man of the Match for Lancashire in 1973 (his county captain, David Lloyd, looks on). *Right* Former adversary turned commentator, Tony Greig, presents the trophy for the World Series Cricket Final in Australia, 1980. *Below* The first World Cup victory – against Australia – at Lord's in 1975.

Above Saluting the fans after receiving the 1975 World Cup from the Duke of Edinburgh.

Below Lloyd's second Prudential World Cup trophy – after the final against England at Lord's in 1979.

Above Clive and Waveney pose on their wedding day for the photographer, Lancashire teammate David Lloyd (September 1971).

Below Several years later: Clive and Waveney with their two daughters.

social relationship between Indians and Afro West Indians in contemporary West Indian society. It goes back a long way.

In the late 1950s politics in Trinidad and in Guyana were split almost entirely along racial lines, Indians versus Negroes. In Trinidad, when Eric Williams, a Doctor of Philosophy and former star Oxford pupil, formed the People's National Movement, perceived as a mainly negroid party, the Indian political elements in society scouted around for a representative with similar educational achievements to lead the Indian opposition party. This was called the Democratic Labour Party and its leader, also a PhD, was Dr Rudrunath Capildeo. With his appointment racial honour was seen to be satisfied.

In Guyana, where memories of slavery are long, there is another factor which keeps Indian–Negro tension alive. Original Amerindians for a time had the job of hunting down runaway slaves. In *The Journal of the British Guiana Museum and Zoo* published in 1960, and based on *The Story of the Slave Rebellion in Berbice in 1762*, there is the following reference:

The aforesaid Indians having brought the expedition to a close, sixty or seventy of them, armed with bow and arrow, returned to Dageraat to report to the Governor, saying that they had scoured the forests throughout, finding eleven negroes whom they had killed, in proof of which they produced a little stick with as many nicks cut in, and asking for some reward. The Governor gave their captains, six in number, each a piece of salamfore, two jugs of rum, some mirrors and other presents, with which being satisfied they returned upcountry.

The Indians who support the Indian cricket team in the West Indies these days are not descendants of Amerindians, although they do get lumped into the general category of having always been anti-Negro. West Indian Indians were brought from India as indentured servants. Their status differed from Negro slaves brought from Africa, who remained slaves until emancipation. In contrast, at the conclusion of their period of indentureship, Indians were freed and given parcels of land.

In his book *From Chattel Slave to Wage Earner*, the Trinidadian writer Ron Ramadhin has this description:

In 1844, it was finally agreed that immigration from India to Trinidad should be effected, permitting the entry of 2,500 Indian

workers from the ports of Calcutta and Madras . . . One third of the
cost of an immigrant's passage to Trinidad plus the possibility of a
return passage following the expiration of his contract, was
financed by public funds in Trinidad . . . East Indian immigration to
Trinidad remained a point of contention until the System of Indenture was abolished in 1917. The East Indian whose term of
Indenture had expired automatically joined the rest of the Island's
free-labour work force . . . they took jobs in agriculture or in
farming, doing much the same work as that performed during their
indentured service. Most of these workers were housed on estates
and in some cases were given plots of land on which sugar cane was
grown, to be sold to their employer . . .

The East Indians thus became early landowners, a status which they
retained and from which much wealth accrued. That wealth which
freed Negro slaves never had the opportunity to acquire was perhaps
one of the greatest causes of social friction between the two groups of
people, so that when East Indians travel to cricket grounds to support
a visiting Indian team there is something of a resurgence of that
residual friction, at times even open hostility. Therefore, while it is
regarded as an international disaster for a West Indies cricket team to
lose against England, to lose to India is to reopen old wounds.

Before 1971 the Indians had never won a Test match against the
West Indies. On the 1971 tour they did better than that. They won the
rubber. The West Indian cricket team, its management and the people
of the islands were thrown into such confusion by this defeat that,
urged on by the media and a host of criticisms from every level of
society, no fewer than twenty players were chosen for the five Tests.
Sobers, Kanhai and Lloyd were the only ones who played in all five
Tests. Lloyd wrily remarks today:

It was one of the more staggering things I have seen. The chopping
and changing was incredible. At one stage, it was possible to draw
lots to guess who your next room-mate was going to be. There was
no direction, no leadership, and most unbelievable of all, there was
a separate manager for each Test match. That must be some kind of
crazy record. It was not just the captaincy. It was everything. Talk
about the doldrums. That was the beginning of our lowest point.

He was right.
Even before the tour began, the captain, Gary Sobers, found himself

in hot water with the government of Guyana. Sobers had gone to
Rhodesia to play in a cricket tournament. Not only was he criticised in
several Caribbean countries, but the Guyana government refused to
allow him into the country to lead the West Indies team. Here was a
complication to end them all. Finally, the West Indies captain expressed his 'sincere regrets' for what he had done and promised never to do
it again. Honour was satisfied and the Guyana Test match was
allowed to go ahead.

Disaster struck the West Indies, though, long before they reached
Georgetown. Sobers had clearly had enough of the West Indies
captaincy, a feeling brought on perhaps by a surfeit of cricket at
international level. His leadership of an ever-changing West Indies
side was bland and uninspiring. India, on the other hand, although at
times much too dour, showed great courage and tremendous fighting
spirit. The course of the Tests taught Clive Lloyd a profound lesson. If
ever the West Indies were to lose to India again, the circumstances
must never be the same if he were to have anything to do with it.

The Indians claimed all the honours in the drawn first Test at Sabina
Park in Kingston. And the match hinged on the opening day's play.
Vanburn Holder, the Barbadian fast bowler, ripped through the upper
half of the Indian batting with four wickets for 60 runs. India were on
the ropes with five wickets down and a mere 75 runs on the board. But
into this Indian batting catastrophe stepped the experienced and stout-
hearted Dilip Sardesai. For just over eight hours he held the West
Indians at bay; he scored 212 runs, the first double century ever by an
Indian batsman against the West Indies and, with commendably able
support from Solkar batting at number seven (he got 61) and Prasanna
at number ten (he scored 25), India soared to the unexpected heights
of 387.

The West Indies began their reply in a state of shock that the best of
their bowlers had been so toyed with by a team not rated as among the
best in the world. The shock waves engulfed their batting. Only
Kanhai reached 50, and having begun the match with the highest
hopes of running through the Indian batting, West Indies were forced
to follow on. It was one of the stranger 'follow-on' incidents in cricket.
The first day's play had been abandoned because of heavy rain. As a
result, the match was reduced to four days and the total required by
the West Indies to avoid having to follow on fell from the customary
200 to 150. What seemed puzzling was the fact that the West Indies
were unaware of this until they were all out for 217.

Batting a second time, a superb innings of 158 not out by Rohan

Kanhai and scores of 93 from Sobers and 57 from Lloyd saved the team from any further indignities. But the West Indies were shaken by the manner in which, after their early loss of wickets on the first day's play, India had held the upper hand. Worse was to follow.

Test matches at the Queen's Park Oval in Port of Spain, Trinidad, are part of the glory of the West Indian game. The setting is exquisite, the ground framed, as if by design, by the towering hills of the northern range. From every part of the country taxis and buses crowd the comparatively narrow thoroughfare leading to the ground. When the Indians play in Trinidad, traffic from the south of the island is particularly heavy. The majority of Trinidad's East Indians live in the southern half of the island. Perhaps nowhere outside of Bombay or Calcutta could an Indian team wish for more support and encouragement. It was, in every way, an appropriate setting for India to make history.

When the West Indies were bowled out for 214, keen cricket statisticians might have suspected that something dramatic was about to happen. It was their lowest-ever score against India. The traditional pattern of matches between the two sides on hard wickets in both India and the Caribbean was that of high scoring and a high proportion of inconclusive games. But facing such a surprisingly low West Indies total this time, India seemed heartened and were transformed into a side sensing an unprecedented opportunity to beat their old rivals. A fine century by Sardesai and sound supporting knocks from Gavaskar, Solkar and Mankad took India well past the West Indies first-innings tally and on to a commanding lead of 138. And yet when the West Indies began their reply, they too seemed ready to respond to the demands of a difficult situation. On the fourth day of the match they had made 150 for the loss of only one wicket. But that was to be their finest moment. They did only slightly better than they had in the first innings and were all out for 261, leaving India to make 124 to win their first Test match against the West Indies. Their batsmen got the runs easily, with Gavaskar acting as the anchor and scoring 67 not out at the close. Indian jubilation was as great as the utter humiliation felt by the West Indies.

Having taken the lead, the Indian captain Wadekar contrived to ensure that nothing should stand in the way of his side's first-ever victory in a series against the West Indies. Several criticisms were levelled against his defensive tactics, but in the end those counted for little. In Guyana, in a high-scoring match in which Lloyd scored 60 out of the West Indies first-innings total of 363, the pitch was much too docile to encourage a result. At Kensington Oval in Barbados, Sobers batted magnificently for 178 not out in the West Indies first-innings score of 501 for 5 declared, but another century for Sardesai made certain a reasonable Indian reply, and having saved the follow-on there was no doubt about the fact that the match would be drawn. So was the last at the Queen's Park Oval in Port of Spain. That final Test was marked by Gavaskar scoring a century and a double century in the same match, and at the end the West Indies, frantically chasing 262 runs to square the series at the rate of six runs an over, not only failed to get them but came perilously close to being defeated when play ended with their score 165 for 8. Lloyd's was one of the better innings; he made 64.

It was [says Clive Lloyd now] every demonstration of how cricket should not be administered. There seemed to be no plan about what to do. Again, there were not a lot of team discussions about what we should do to restore the situation. I think I learnt a great deal from that series. It taught me that cricket has to be played with the utmost professionalism. It's not possible to depend on things just happening even with the greatest sides. And we obviously weren't, since there had been so much chopping and changing. The other important point was that managers can be important and to think that we could have a different manager in each Test venue was madness. I suppose that in that way it was a great lesson for us. We never quite deteriorated to that again.

On a more personal level, it was the beginning of a most frustrating period. Three times in five innings I was run out, and somehow you sense that things aren't going quite right, that the team isn't pulling together as a team when that happens. I learnt a lot from that; about the way cricket teams should be run. Looking back, it was a bad time.

Every island seemed to come up with its own solution about what should be done to rescue the West Indies team from disgrace. Trinidad wanted their man, Joey Carew, to replace Sobers; Jamaicans had another view, Barbados was saying this and that, 'get rid of this one and that one'. It was West Indian insularity at its worst. I have hardly known a team with a lower morale with all the confusion going on around it.

And there was considerable confusion too on the field of play. I was run out twice in the first Test, on one occasion when I was really playing well, hitting the ball cleanly in the middle of the bat and past

50. I had got to the 60s in the third Test and it was the same thing again. And then I collided with Sobers in full flight.

The lack of any appreciation of what was going on was also stunning. To think that when in the first Test the follow-on margin had been reduced from 220 to 150, no one in the West Indies camp were aware. That was really incredible. And then in the last Test in Port of Spain, there was an even more bizarre incident.

Gary and Wadekar went out to toss, Gary spun the coin and the Indian skipper said he would bat. Gary was surprised, because he was sure that Wadekar had called wrongly. And that view was supported by a few people who were looking on at close quarters. So you had both captains claiming the toss. Instead of agreeing to settle the matter by spinning the coin again, Gary simply shrugged his shoulders and let the Indians bat. And that was the last Test match, the one we had to win to square the series. Some people called it sportsmanship on Gary's part, but for my money it was not cricket. No one would get away with that from me. It's not professional. It does not amount to trying your best to win for your side. But it was typical of the disarray we were in.

I remember one team meeting, when a respected Trinidadian cricket figure, Lance Pierre, our match manager, came up with the brilliant suggestion that perhaps the way to get Gavaskar's wicket cheaply might be to bring him on the front foot, bowl him full tosses at waist height, and because of his anxiety to get the ball away, there was a good chance that he'll give a catch to deep square-leg. That says it all. That was the level to which we had sunk. And it made me realise just how badly the whole game was being run and how important it was to change that. I suppose I secretly vowed then that if I had anything to do with it, it would never revert to those dark days. All these incidents taught me a lot and shaped my captaincy of the West Indies team much later.

Life did improve for Lloyd in the months immediately following the Indian tour. Lancashire won an exciting Gillette Cup Final at Lord's in 1971 and he had been among the runs. He comfortably passed a thousand runs for the season and played a hard-hitting knock against Warwickshire, ending up with 217 not out.

But then tragedy. An injury to his spine in Australia, when he was playing for a World team, kept him in hospital for a month, anxiously wondering whether he would ever be able to play the game again.

Lloyd missed the first three Tests against the visiting New Zealanders in the West Indies in 1971–72 but was selected for the fourth on his home ground in Guyana. The match ended in a draw, but Lloyd's memory of it has more to do with the fact that he was again run out, this time for 43. The Guyana crowd, beginning to believe that something of a conspiracy theory was operating against their local hero, were so annoyed that some sections threw bottles on to the field. Calm was restored only when Lloyd himself appealed to the spectators over the local radio.

Feeling his way back into Test cricket after his injury, Lloyd's contribution to the final Test in a most dispiriting series of five drawn games against New Zealand was minimal. He made 18 and 5. But he was totally unprepared for what happened next.

My form [he says] was not the best, obviously. But I was getting back into shape after the lay-off. So you could imagine my shock when I learnt that I had not been selected for the 1973 series against the Australians at home. I was terribly angry and hurt by that and decided to accept an invitation to play club cricket in Australia. Before that, though, the selectors were terribly embarrassed by the fact that at the end of the 1972 season in England Lancashire won the Gillette Cup again and the Man of the Match award went to none other than C. H. Lloyd. I scored 126.

Embarrassed the West Indies selectors certainly were. The English newspapers the day after the Gillette Cup Final at Lord's were uniformly ecstatic about Lloyd's batting. His innings was described in purple prose as one of the best ever seen in one-day competitions. One writer called it one of the finest demonstrations of aggressive and brilliant strokeplay seen at Lord's. The English crowd had hailed Lloyd as a hero, and when he was called forward to receive the Man of the Match award the acclamation could be heard halfway round London.

What followed was typical of the confused way West Indies cricket has sometimes been run. Although Gary Sobers had relinquished the captaincy, no successor had been named and, in the absence of that, speculation was rife. As usual every island had its own contender, but most peculiar of all was the fact that Lloyd was one name quite openly and consistently canvassed. But how could he be captain when he had not even been selected for the Australian tour?

A modicum of order was restored to the situation when Lloyd was cabled by the West Indies Board and requested to stand by for the visit of the Australians since Sobers was recovering from an operation and his fitness was in doubt. Neither the people nor for that matter the government of Guyana were terribly pleased about Lloyd's exclusion from the original team; the Guyanese Prime Minister, Forbes Burnham, had personally intervened by asking his friend, the Australian Prime Minister, Gough Whitlam, to make sure that there would be no problem getting Lloyd's release from his commitment to club cricket in Australia. Guyana wanted Lloyd standing by in the Caribbean. And Mr Burnham went further. Back in Manchester, Lloyd was informed through the Guyanese High Commission in London that his country had decided to pay his fare back to the Caribbean. He was deeply disturbed about the implications of political interference in what was essentially a sporting matter, but decided nevertheless to go back to Guyana.

Lloyd adds:

> The point about it was that my Prime Minister made a request that I come back home and I found it impossible to refuse and certainly I wanted to be near the action. I was sure omitting me from the original selection was a mistake and I was quite desperate to have a chance to prove the selectors wrong. But my problems were only just beginning. I was named in the squad for the first Test, but didn't make the team. Then I was named in the twelve for the second Test in Barbados and just before the start of play I was told that I would be twelfth man. That almost precipitated the end of my career with the West Indies. I was mad. I hit a ball through a dressing-room window, stormed off the practice pitch where I was when I was told I would not be playing, and out of sheer frustration cried my eyes out in the dressing-room. Now all I wanted to do was to get back to England. It seemed to me at the time that the action of the Guyana government in bringing me back to the Caribbean had embarrassed the West Indies selectors, who were now intent on getting their own back. The one way was to humiliate me. I decided I couldn't stand for it and wanted out. I refused to be twelfth man, refused to take part in the shaking of hands with the Governor-General before the match. But, of course, a few wiser heads counselled caution. I think that even then some people saw my true potential.

Wes Hall, the team manager, calmly pointed out to Lloyd that Kanhai, who by then had replaced Sobers as West Indies captain, could only be an interim leader as his playing career was nearing its end. And in Hall's view that would leave the way open for Lloyd to press his claims for the captaincy of the side. Fortunately for himself and for West Indies cricket, Lloyd listened to Wes Hall, fulfilled his duties as twelfth man during the second Test, and kept his place in the squad. Selected for the Trinidad Test, he struggled painfully for runs and was rounded on by the Trinidad crowd for his poor showing. That began a long feud between Clive Lloyd and Trinidad's cricket followers.

More than ten years later, *Challenge Newspaper*, a racy Trinidadian journal, openly accused the West Indies captain of attempting to get Trinidad by-passed as a Test venue. The paper wrote: 'West Indies captain, Clive Lloyd, has made it abundantly clear that he is not prepared to play in Trinidad and Tobago ever again. "I am not prepared to go to that country as West Indies captain to play," he was quoted as saying.' The article went on to assert that Lloyd had apparently persuaded other members of the West Indies team that it was much more rewarding to play Test cricket before crowds in other West Indian islands.

Lloyd strenuously denies ever having said that and publicly called the article 'inaccurate and containing no factual basis whatever'. He went on to say: 'Having read the piece, I consider it to be a personal attack not only against me, but against the other members of the West Indies team.'

The affair itself is perhaps a matter of little real importance. But it gives an interesting insight into the fierce national loyalties which characterised West Indies team selection up until very recently. Trinidadians disapproved of what they felt was the Guyana government's attempt to influence the Test selectors by having Lloyd flown back to the Caribbean. The fact that the Prime Minister himself became involved only strengthened the view that there had been political interference at the highest level. When Lloyd made the team and failed to get many runs in the Trinidad Test match, his head was well and truly on the chopping-block. But even more to the point is the fact that a Trinidadian player, Charlie Davis, who had scored many runs for the West Indies in 1972 and 1973, had been dropped from the team for the first three Test matches against the Australians. And, led by Trinidadian sports writers and commentators, the public were encouraged to form the view that Lloyd's return spoilt the chances of the young Trinidad star.

Lloyd's personal problems had occurred against a backdrop of turmoil in West Indian cricket. And the Australian tour itself provided a dramatic illustration of that condition. Before the Australians arrived, the West Indies had played 26 Test matches and had won only two of them. Even more depressing had been the fact that they had been beaten by India and had failed to beat New Zealand, two of the weakest Test countries, and both at home.

The mood which surrounded West Indies Test performances was one of deep melancholy by the time Ian Chappell brought his team to the Caribbean. There had been a row about Sobers, who was unfit for the first Test, indicated that he was able to play in the second, but was ruled out by the West Indies selectors unless he underwent a fitness test at an exhibition match. The great man considered this a stain on his reputation and refused. His absence was keenly felt.

The first two Test matches against the Australians at Kingston and Bridgetown in February and March 1973 were drawn, and at the Queen's Park Oval in Port of Spain, where Lloyd failed, Australia won by 46 runs. Two weeks later in the fourth Test at Bourda in Guyana, Australia's superiority over a struggling West Indian team was even more emphatically demonstrated. This time, Chappell's team won by ten wickets. But the match marked Lloyd's return to form, although this was the only small bright spot in an overall picture of unmitigated gloom. The West Indian cricket writer and commentator, Tony Cozier, said of the last two Test matches and of Lloyd's batting:

> The hero of the first day of the fourth Test was unquestionably Lloyd. With Prime Minister Burnham basking in reflected glory, the loose-limbed left-hander reinstated himself in the team and erased doubts about his real merit as a Test player. Abandoning the contact lenses he used in the previous Test match and reverting to spectacles, Lloyd was in irresistible mood, attacking confidently and hitting a six and twenty-four fours before he was out on the second morning for 178. He added a record 187 for the fourth wicket with the West Indies captain, Rohan Kanhai, but no one else scored more than 30, and on the second day of the Test match the last seven West Indian wickets fell for a miserable 89 runs.

Australia won that Test match easily. Cozier continues:

> A pall of gloom descended over West Indies cricket, a predictable culmination of the discord which had affected it in so many ways throughout the season. Its manifestation was seen in the final meaningless Test at the Queen's Park Oval in Port of Spain. When

the third Test had been played there, 90,000 people all told had watched five gripping days of cricket; now a tenth of that total turned up to see the final rites to the series. Some days, barely 1,000 were present. West Indians, it seemed, had had enough of the buffeting which their national sport had suffered both on and off the field.

Clive Lloyd adds:

It was a most depressing time, but we were soon on the mend. Kanhai turned out to be a conscientious captain, not as daring as Sobers, and many times a little too defensive, but at least we had a captain who had not lost his appetite for leadership. We began to talk about our problems at team meetings and there was a better spirit among the team members. After losing to the Australians, we came to England and won convincingly. And my form returned.

It is an understatement merely to say that Lloyd's form returned. His batting dominated the three-match series against England in 1973.

In the first Test at the Oval he went out to bat with the West Indies score at 64 for 3 and the England seamers, Geoff Arnold and John Snow, getting considerable movement in the air and off the pitch. But Lloyd and Kallicharran mounted a memorable rescue act, putting on over 200 for the fourth wicket. Lloyd went on to score 132 before a wildly enthusiastic West Indian contingent at the Oval, his first Test hundred in England.

At Edgbaston he failed to reach a second century by six runs, and he scored 63 in the final match at Lord's. On the tour as a whole he scored 1,128 runs in 23 innings for an average of just under 60.

By the time he next played for the West Indies in England, he was captain.

CHAPTER SIX
'Hubert' Takes Command

When the news was confirmed that I had been made captain, I was in a word . . . thunderstruck.

C. H. Lloyd

When we see him bat, bowl or field we know he is not an English player, not an Australian player . . . We know that his cuts and drives . . . are consequences of impulses born in the blood, a blood heated by the sun . . . impulses not common to the psychology of the over-civilised places on the earth.

Neville Cardus, describing
Learie Constantine

With the notable exception of Frank Worrell, no West Indian cricket captain has ever given as much thought to the nature and requirements of the job as Clive Lloyd has.

Gary Sobers had never been a thoughtful leader. He was made captain of the West Indies side because he was the greatest all-round player of his day. The captaincy fell into his hands, naturally. He saw no need to set himself goals. He was already in the process of surpassing any he might have set by the time he became captain. And no other player of the day could be compared to him. He was neither long-term planner nor strategist. Neither was deemed necessary. He never gave a thought to the fact that players needed encouragement, inspiration. His was a free-ranging genius with scant regard for discipline. In his own view, and perhaps quite correctly, his batting – his truculently masterful strokeplay, his bowling – quick or slow with that unique loose-limbed action, his fielding – apparently relaxed yet so deadly alert, provided all the encouragement, all the inspiration any team could need. Sobers captained the West Indies team as a man apart. He would desert his men just before Test matches and feel no necessity to talk with his players about how a game should be approached. Why, if the side was ever in trouble, the world's greatest player would certainly come to the rescue!

The former England player, Tom Graveney, remembers with great wit and warmth the Sobers approach to Test cricket:

It was not terribly difficult to read what Gary would do. Of course, we never knew whether he'd make 40 or 200 or whether he'd decide to bowl out the opposition, but he was in some respects predictable. If Gary got a century, then we knew he would not be opening the bowling. He'd probably be first change, or he might even wait a little longer and try his slower stuff. But if Gary failed to make runs, then we could be absolutely sure that he was going to take the new ball, and although he was never as fast as some of the West Indies pace bowlers of his day, we knew his tail would be up and he would be deadly. Gary ran the game. He hardly needed a team. That, perhaps, was the beginning and end of his strategy. Now, in any discussion about whether or not he was a great captain, you could take your choice, but you were dealing with the greatest player in the world. That made a big difference. He was always the one man capable of changing the course of a match dramatically. None of his successors can claim to have been able to do that to the extent to which it was true of Sobers.

Under Sobers, the West Indies team never reached anything like its full potential. There is very little evidence to suggest that much professional thought went into the possibility of realising that.

The brilliant Guyanese batsman, Rohan Kanhai, who succeeded Sobers as captain for a short time, tried his best to open up the lines of communication to his team. He was not a great communicator, however, and many of his team did not quite know what to make of him; while some of the cricket the West Indies played under him looked dour and totally defensive at times, Kanhai himself could personally be very aggressive. When, during the 1973 tour of England, umpire Arthur Fagg refused to uphold an appeal by the West Indian players for a caught-behind against Boycott, it was Kanhai, not his younger, wilder players, who led the feet-stamping protests. Umpire Fagg had refused to take the field the following day until the West Indian team formally apologised.

But even more to the point was the fact that Kanhai never held the job of West Indian captain for long enough. His was generally viewed as an interim arrangement, almost attempting to fill the hiatus, the vacuum after the departure of the great Sobers. And perhaps Kanhai knew this.

From the outset Clive Lloyd felt differently about his appointment to the job. He had the perspicacity to realise that if he showed the necessary leadership and if he got the right results he could be at the

64   CLIVE LLOYD

helm of his country's cricket for a considerable time. He saw the potential in the job and having been in the West Indian team for a number of years, at times when West Indies cricket had been torn by factional discord and when it had suffered disastrously from lack of professionalism, he felt he had a pretty shrewd idea what was needed if the side was to become a winning combination. But the most significant point about Lloyd's being made captain was the fact that he had given the matter the most serious thought; he made a careful assessment of the problems facing the West Indian game, and he mapped out in broad outline what he would do and the course his captaincy would take.

He had not had a great deal of practical experience in the captaincy field. He had led teams in Guyana occasionally, and when his Lancashire namesake and captain David Lloyd had been needed to play for England he had captained the county side. But he was beginning to believe that his own success had been due not so much to experience as to natural talent allied to a thoughtful, professional approach. There is perhaps no greater evidence of this fact than to remember that Clive Lloyd, the batsman, has never had a coaching lesson in his life. His game is his own. He fashioned his batting on what he had seen in his youth. And then he picked up a bat and began to play as we know him today. Adjustments in style and the ability to play certain bowlers better have come along the way, but Lloyd plays and bats almost identically to the way he did 25 years ago. (He has always regarded coaching with something close to disdain. And he blames some English coaching for encouraging batsmen to be much too defensive. Told once that his feet were not in the correct position after he had executed a shot, Lloyd replied: 'I'm not interested where my *feet* are as long as the *ball* is racing to the boundary.') So he would also bring to the captaincy, not the distilled wisdom of others, but his own views. It was the way his career in the game had developed.

Kanhai's West Indian team beat England in 1973, but England came from behind to level an indifferent series in the West Indies the following winter. Lloyd had a particularly poor home season. He only once managed to reach 50. With a tour of India, Sri Lanka and Pakistan to come later in the year, the West Indies decided to relieve Kanhai of the captaincy and to appoint C. H. Lloyd in his place. Lloyd recalls:

In the first place, I simply didn't believe that I would be given the job. And then, when it was confirmed, I was thunderstruck. It was, of course, a tremendous honour. It took some time for the word to come officially from the West Indies Board, but I heard the news when I was rung up by the *Daily Mirror*'s cricket correspondent, Howard Booth. Lancashire were in the middle of a Roses match. It was not possible to do much celebrating then, but I certainly made up for it when I went down to London a few days later.

When the news sank in, I came to believe that in appointing me the West Indies were looking for some kind of long-term leadership of the team. It seemed to me that it was not in their minds to have a stop-gap captain. So I decided that the job of leading the West Indies should be taken with the utmost seriousness and I set myself a number of goals. The first priority was clearly the need for team unity. We couldn't expect good results if we were always fighting among ourselves and bickering. I decided I had to try to put this over to the players forcefully. I tried to emphasise at the same time how much I wanted them to play for me. I believe it's about the most important thing. A captain must so inspire his players that they always try, they always want to do their best for whoever is in charge. If you get that, you're on to a winner. If you don't, there's a lack of firm loyalty and you might not achieve such good results.

In return, I was able to offer them assurances that I would work to improve their position. I started out from the premise that I wanted West Indies cricket and West Indies cricketers to be treated with respect. So I told the players I would fight for better conditions for them. I wanted them to portray a different image. We had been for a long time thought of as happy-go-lucky cricketers, who are great when the game's going our way, but who fold when things get tough. That image had to change. I was determined to play hard, to instill a new professionalism in our approach. I wanted the West Indies to be a winning team, to be successful. I wanted to win as captain, and to win for the honour of West Indies cricket, and of the West Indies nation. That's very important. I know that Bob Willis in his book and other people have said that in wanting to win so badly, I became cruel. I don't accept that, but as captain I developed the killer instinct. Nice guys never rule the world. That didn't mean that gentlemanly sportsmanship had to suffer. You could play the game hard, be professional, tough and yet be very fair. That's what I was determined to strive for. There is nothing like being a good loser. Much later in my career, Kerry Packer used to say, the only good loser is the one who loses often. I didn't want that to be me. I was determined to be a winner.

Lancashire won no honours in 1974, but what with the occasional responsibility of leading the county side and being asked to become captain of the West Indies, it was a most memorable season for Lloyd. He had again been in sparkling form with the bat. He scored four centuries during the season, his highest being 178 not out, but more to the point was the fact that he had consistently been among the runs. 40s and 50s were invariably against his name. His tally for the summer was 1,458 runs for an average of just over 63, which put him top of the averages for the season.

In India in 1974–75, the West Indies won an exciting series by three Test matches to two in such a manner that many of the criticisms of earlier encounters were silenced. For the first time in nearly two decades, the West Indies had gone into a series without those two famous names Sobers and Kanhai, but as Lloyd himself points out, the most encouraging aspect of the Indian tour was the fact that the West Indies mounted a magnificent team effort. It was just the tonic the new captain was looking for.

> Everybody made a contribution [says Lloyd], that's what I set out to achieve. I was lucky on my first tour as captain to have Gerry Alexander as manager. He helped us to get good team discussions going, at times playing devil's advocate to elicit views from the players. It was a good spirit. And the results spoke for themselves. We didn't crush India or Pakistan. But our five major batsmen all got runs – over 300. Even those who didn't play in all the Tests weighed in with centuries when it was important. Our bowlers did well. It was a great start to my captaincy. And I felt we were beginning to develop that team unity I so badly wanted.

Lloyd himself was in tremendous form with the bat. If assuming the captaincy can sometimes affect a player's performance, it certainly wasn't so in his case. His contribution to the first Test against India in Bangalore, which the West Indies won by a massive 267 runs, was a splendid score of 163. In the second Test in Delhi, he partnered Richards for a while, advising him how to play the Indian spinners and seeing the Antiguan reach his first century in Test cricket. (He went on to make 192 not out.) Lloyd's knock produced a patient 71. And at the Wankhede Stadium in Bombay in the final Test, Lloyd's batting reached its irrepressible best. He took total command of the Indian attack. He played the spinners with caution, but was murderous on anything short. He repeatedly lifted loose deliveries out of the ground and went on to make 242 not out, his highest score in any grade of cricket. On the way he put on 250 runs with Deryck Murray for the West Indies sixth wicket, a new record. His aggregate for the series against India was 636 runs, his highest in a Test series. Against Pakistan he scored 164 runs in three innings. No worries about the burdens of leadership here; rather, evidence of a player who positively revelled in the challenge of his new job. The biggest challenge of his cricket life came in the following year, and Clive Lloyd was more than equal to it. Before the end of 1975 his batting had inspired Lancashire to a memorable Gillette Cup victory at Lord's and he had led the West Indies to the summit of international cricket.

Always proud of his association with Lancashire, Lloyd's form during the summer of 1975 was the talking-point of the county's performance. He scored 1423 runs during that summer, including six hundreds, a record he was never to better. His batting average over 18 matches was 61. And his innings of 73 not out against Middlesex in the Gillette Cup Final at Lord's helped his captain David Lloyd to win a major trophy for the first time.

David Lloyd says of that game:

I have two memories of the match. The first is that when Clive had scored about 40 he mistimed a shot off the Middlesex offspinner Freddie Titmus and was dropped by, of all people, Mike Smith.

I was terrified when that ball was in the air, because had he been caught out then, we would have been in a desperate state. We might just have held on to win the game, but it would have been difficult.

So I stalked down the wicket to tell him that he must be more careful. But in the heat of the match I obviously did it in a very agitated manner, because my second memory of that match is the fact that when it was all over, and we were in the middle of celebrating our victory, my friends told me how ridiculous I looked staring up at the big man and wagging my finger at him, admonishing him not to repeat any dangerous shots such as the one off Titmus. It must have made the funniest picture.

Of Learie Constantine, Neville Cardus wrote many years ago:

When we see him bat, bowl or field, we know he is not an English player, not an Australian player, not a South African player. We know that his cuts and drives, his leapings and clutchings and dartings – we know that they are the consequences of impulses born in the blood, a blood heated by the sun and influenced by an environment and way of life much more natural than ours; impulses not common to the psychology of the over-civilised places on the earth.

David Lloyd believes that the same description applies today to Clive Lloyd.

His big hitting defied any description. No England player, no other player anywhere has hit the ball like Clive to my way of thinking. He's such a big man. I will never forget one match against Surrey. I think we lost that one, yet the enduring memory is of a big hit by Clive. Robin Jackman was the bowler. In fairness to Robin, it must be said that he slipped as he was about to deliver the ball. But Lloydie spotted that Jackman had slipped, and lunged into the delivery. He struck it a mighty blow. We seemed to watch it and watch it and watch it . . . it seemed never to stop rising, it cleared the ground and landed across the road against Archbishop Tenison's Grammar School even further away. I have never seen a hit like that. That is a West Indian hit. Nobody else playing cricket can do that kind of thing.

In one John Player League match we were in a spot of bother, fell further behind in the asking rate and were left to get something like ten an over when Lloydie came in. To tell the truth, even with Clive in the side, I had given up any hopes for the match. I think we all had. But not the big man. It was against Middlesex and Clive set about their bowlers like a man possessed. He hit everything so cleanly, but even when he didn't, the ball tended to sail over the boundary – most infuriating to their bowlers. Single-handedly Clive got us the runs and to the consternation of Middlesex we won that match.

David Lloyd says that the mild-mannered Clive could be an even more ferocious hitter when roused.

We were playing Gloucester at Old Trafford in the Gillette Cup; we were chasing 267 and not doing terribly well at something like 30 for 3. Clive and I were at the wicket. Mike Procter bowled one at him, Clive had an almighty whack at it but didn't quite get hold of it. But he's such a powerful man that the ball flew off the edge and carried over the boundary ropes for six. Procter was livid with rage and must have said a few unpleasant things to Clive or about him in his hearing. I don't think it was anything more than a bowler's frustration. But it annoyed Clive. I walked down the wicket to talk to him to try to calm him down, but he just looked at me and said: 'That man is vexing me. I'm going to hit him over the pavilion.' I simply told him to make sure he connected well. And he did. The very next ball from Procter, who was not the easiest player to get away, Clive hit him over the pavilion. It was a magnificent hit. And not only that, Clive and I stayed and we won the match from being three down for thirty-odd chasing 267. We put on 234 runs together, establishing then a new one-day record.

Clive Lloyd's former Lancashire team-mate, friend and business partner, Jack Simmons, cannot commend too highly the contribution Lloyd has made to Lancashire cricket. (Together they have formed a consultancy to try to find places in county cricket for overseas players wanting to play in England.)
Simmons says:

He is without question the greatest thing that has ever happened to Lancashire cricket in my lifetime. It is the most marvellous thing to sit in the pavilion and hear the buzz of excitement and feel the atmosphere as Clive takes those long loping steps down the pavilion stairs and out onto the ground to the wicket. The crowd stirs in anticipation; they know and we know we're privileged to be in the presence of one of the greats. No one else has his power, his strokeplay. He's always had a sense of occasion for Lancashire. He's made runs when they've been most needed. But he's also the most unselfish player you would find in the game today. He is essentially a team man through and through. I've been captain on occasions when he has gone after quick runs, sacrificing his wicket in the process, because that's what was required of the team. He thinks of the team and has never put personal records or averages above playing for the team. And he's been the most dedicated player with whom I've ever been associated. In one Gillette Cup quarter-final against Surrey, Clive had been having trouble with his knees and by the time he arrived at the ground he could hardly move. He sat in the dressing-room in obvious discomfort, so much so that when I met Jim Laker about an hour before the match and he asked whether I had any changes in my team, I told him that Clive was injured and would not play.

Back in the dressing-room, Clive asked me whether I would bowl a few at him. I said I would, but it was pathetic to see him try to get up and to descend the stairs one at a time, just like a paralysed old man. In the nets he loosened up a little and then insisted that he should play. He said it was a crucial game, and he didn't want to let the side down. And Clive went out there and batted in great pain, scoring a match-saving 70 runs before lunch. During lunch his knees tightened up again and he crawled out of the dressing-room to resume his innings. And then, failing to get forward to a ball from Pat Pocock, he was bowled. By that time, the pain had become too great. I know few county players of whatever nationality who would do that for a side. But that's Clive.

That game convinced Lloyd that he could no longer continue playing without an operation on his legs.

It had got to the point where it was very painful and very difficult to move, let alone play shots. So I had both cartilages removed and that relieved the pain and the pressure a great deal. But it did mean that I was never able to swoop about in the covers any more and it also restricted my bowling. And so in county and international cricket I started to field at first-slip. The key to that is keeping your eye on the ball, and having some kind of understanding with the wicket-keeper. Some keepers are divers, they go for everything, and some are not. Neither is a great problem, so long as first-slip knows what the keeper will do. If the keeper moves and then changes his mind, the man at first-slip suddenly finds the ball on him, and he will be very lucky to be able to hold it. Sometimes you manage to hold on to the ball, but the force, when it's not properly caught, could result in injury. I have more than once broken bones in my hands, sometimes without knowing it at the time, because of not taking the ball cleanly.

But Lloyd's team-mate Jack Simmons has the final word:

Despite the fact that he was happier at first-slip after his operation, I remember one occasion when we were in a spot of trouble and I desperately wanted Clive to bowl. He simply said: 'If you want me to bowl, I'll give you a few overs.' And he bowled eight overs very economically and got us out of a tight spot. That's what I call the ultimate in professionalism and unselfishness. There can be no greater team player than Clive.

Simmons also praises Lloyd's interest in helping young up-and-coming players, especially players from the West Indies who must find places in professional cricket in England or Australia. Sometime in 1983, Lloyd saw a young Jamaican quick bowler, Patrick Balfour Patterson, and implored Simmons to try to find him a place in England or Tasmania, where Simmons himself played. After Lloyd had made several calls from various parts of the West Indies insisting what a good find Patterson was, Simmons managed to get the young Jamaican on to the Lancashire staff.

It is [he says] the hallmark of a really big man. His interest in the game has always extended beyond his own personal performance or future. He has been devoted to Lancashire cricket and his interest in the development and future of West Indies cricket is as profound as you could want. He really cares about it and that is why so many people would like him to be permanently associated with West Indies cricket.

The former Lancashire captain and current manager, Jack Bond, says that when it was announced that the county would be taking on two overseas players – Clive Lloyd and the Indian wicket-keeper Farouk Engineer – the press in Manchester wondered above all how two overseas players would fit into an all-white county side.

It was really strange [says Bond]. That's all they could think about. What we Lancashire players worried about was how nine county players would be able to match up to the performances of two great international players. That was our concern. If I could find players born in the county with Clive's dedication to our cricket, we would be the most successful county in the country. Yes, I would say that Clive showed that he cared more for the county than players who were born in it.

Bond's judgement is shared by everyone who has followed Lloyd's performances for the county. He had made his début for Lancashire against the Australians in 1968 and, as his team-mates testify, he played a significant part in restoring the success which the club had longed for through most of the 1950s and 1960s.

When Lancashire beat Sussex in 1970 to win the Gillette Cup, Lloyd made 29 runs and took one wicket, but he also played his part in the field. One reporter covering the game said: 'What really seemed to

rattle Sussex at a crucial point in the game was the presence of Clive
Lloyd in the covers. Lloyd's presence alone was almost entirely
responsible for three otherwise quite unnecessary run-outs.'

One year later, in the 1971 Gillette Cup Final at Lord's, he easily
topped Lancashire's scoring with an impeccable 66. Lancashire had
begun badly, losing Barry Wood before he had scored. But Lloyd held
the innings together and Jack Bond's side were able to reach 224 and
safety in their battle with Kent.

On 4 September 1972, Lloyd was back at Lord's as Lancashire
reached the final of the Gillette Cup competition for the third time in as
many years. It was a wonderful day, a packed ground bathed in the
warmth of late summer sunshine and the occasion of Jack Bond's last
final in his retirement season.

E. W. Swanton described Lloyd's contribution in that final against
Warwickshire thus:

If any man won a match for his side, Clive Lloyd did so for
Lancashire. Coming in when they had lost both openers for 26 after
ten overs . . . he was forced to begin with uncharacteristic restraint.
After eight overs, he'd made only six. But then he drove Brown with
a rare crack past mid-on, and pulled the next ball for six to square-
leg. These strokes set him off and from then onwards it seemed to
matter little to him who bowled what. With strokes of elemental
power, this large, lithe man hit the ball at a speed which on the fast
outfield time and again made cutting off impossible. There were an
unusual number of boundaries for Cup Cricket in Lloyd's innings of
126, 14 fours and three sixes, and the whole marvellous performance lasted only two and a half hours or 42 overs.
    Whereas Lancashire needed to make almost four an over, Lloyd
scored three an over off his own bat. And to consider that in the
absence of both Lever and Shuttleworth, neither of whom was
chosen to play for Lancashire, Lloyd opened the bowling and
confined Warwickshire in his 12 overs to 31 runs, it is clear that no
one has ever won a Man of the Match award by such a large margin.

When, in 1974 in the Gillette Cup Final against Kent, Clive Lloyd
was Lancashire's top scorer with only 25, his team slumped to 118 in
their 60 overs and were easily overhauled by Kent. The decisive
moment for Lancashire had come when Lloyd, going well and looking
as though he was about to repeat his previous Gillette Cup performances, played Johnson off his legs, took one run and looked for a

second as Ealham at deep square cut off the four. Kennedy called 'No'; Lloyd had only four yards or so to regain his ground, but as he turned the big man slipped and fell and although he hurled himself at the crease he failed to beat the excellent return from the deep. With that fall Lancashire's chances of getting a respectable total seemed to end.

In a memorable game against Derbyshire the following season, Lancashire overwhelmed the understrength Midlands team at Buxton. Derbyshire were routed twice within three and a half hours for 42 and 87 in reply to Lancashire's merciless first-innings score of 477 for 5. The man who did most of the damage to Derbyshire's pride was Clive Lloyd, who made 167 not out including eight sixes and 16 fours. In 22 overs, he and Simmons put on 171 before a halt was called to the onslaught.

With Lancashire in the Gillette Cup Final again at Lord's in 1975, there was a distinct sense that yet another Lancashire victory, their fourth in six years, was almost inevitable. David Lloyd won the toss and sent Middlesex in to bat. They began with quiet confidence, but slumped quickly to 33 for 3, were six wickets down for 117, and from that point on never looked like getting a big score. In their 60 overs they could only manage 180 runs.

Lancashire lost opener Barry Wood for 13 and Frank Hayes, batting at number three, for 17, and were 55 for 2 when Lloyd strode out to bat and to take control. Almost immediately he drove the field back with the power of his shots; he ran his singles faster and with a few well-chosen and massive drives, including a magnificent pull off Phil Edmonds, he settled the issue with overs to spare.

Tony Greig made Lloyd the Man of the Match for his 73 not out and the lasting memory of a great summer's cricket remained the sight and sound of a tall, bespectacled left-handed West Indian batsman swinging a huge bat and despatching the ball to the furthest corners of almost every cricket ground in the country. (Incidentally, the bat's general weight in recent years has been 2 lb 2 or 3 ounces; Clive's weighs 2 lb 11½ ounces and is fortified by three rubber handle grips. Even if an average player can lift Clive's bat he would find it difficult to get his hands round the handle.)

In that memorable 1975 season for Lancashire, Clive Lloyd scored six centuries and six fifties in making 1,423 runs and taking 18 catches, and he was happy to play his part in Lancashire's success. But uppermost in the minds of all West Indians and in the mind of the new West Indies captain was that year's World Cup. There had never been a competition like it before, bringing together all the cricket-playing nations of the world for a one-day knockout competition. Nothing could be more important to the cricket followers in the West Indies. For decades, through the years of failure and success, they had harboured the deep-seated belief that their cricket team was the best in the world, and especially in limited-over competitions. Here now was a chance to prove it. The pressure on the new captain to deliver was intense. 'And,' says Lloyd, 'the competition was to produce some of the most exciting cricket I have ever taken part in. I have never known such an atmosphere in a West Indies dressing-room. Let's face it, we had something to prove. If we were the best one-day competition players, this was the chance.'

The pressure on Lloyd and the West Indies to do well was hardly eased by the fact that the West Indies were made early favourites to win the World Cup, although Lloyd had always maintained, and said so at the time, that England at home were never an easy proposition. The West Indies had been bracketed in their section with Australia, Pakistan and the newcomers to full international status, Sri Lanka. Victory against Sri Lanka was accomplished without too many alarms and while all eyes were on a fixture in the other group (comprising England, India, New Zealand and East Africa) the West Indies journeyed to Edgbaston to play Pakistan. It almost turned out to be the end of their World Cup hopes.

Pakistan, who were never underestimated by the West Indies, batted first and got off to a fine start. Lloyd says: 'We didn't bowl as well as we might have and of course the Pakistanis have a number of splendid and stylish players. So they scored a little more than we had bargained for and from that moment on we had a fight on our hands.'

But not even the West Indian skipper could anticipate then just how great a battle his team had on its hands. It had been a perfect day, conditions were ideal for batting, and, given the strength of the West Indian strokemakers, no one gave Pakistan very much of a chance. But very soon a hush descended on the ground at Birmingham. The first three wickets went cheaply. Lloyd himself failed to get going and, chasing 267, the West Indies found themselves tottering 100 runs behind and with only two wickets left. 166 for 8 was the score when Vanburn Holder, better known as an accurate fast bowler than as a batsman, strode out to the middle to join Deryck Murray, who was defending as though his life depended on it. Holder tried, but couldn't stay with Murray long enough to make his innings count. When he went, Andy Roberts joined Murray. Surely now the Pakistanis could not be denied. Clive Lloyd was certain at this point that his team had blown their chances. 'Yes,' he admits, 'I thought we were beaten. I began to look back on the match and saw our mistakes. We could have bowled tighter, more accurately, and our batting had failed. That adds up very simply to defeat. I was sure we were out of it.'

But for once the West Indian captain was wrong. Gradually, the Murray–Roberts partnership began to upset their opponents. Pakistan's fluent cricket began to show visible signs of panic; Murray was as solid as a rock and Roberts proved a clean, efficient hitter. He pushed to leg, when he didn't drive ambitiously through the offside. At the other end Murray seemed to have all the time in the world to angle his bat to avoid the Pakistan fielders. As the Pakistanis panicked, the two West Indians appeared calmer and more confident. With two balls to go, Andy Roberts turned a delivery from Wasim Raja backward of square and began the desperate, joyful scamper to the pavilion to evade the hordes of West Indian supporters who came pouring onto the field to embrace two unlikely West Indian heroes and to acclaim a famous escape. 'West Indies Houdini act' cried the sports headline the following day, and no one could challenge that.

It was [says Lloyd] just about the most emotional moment in my career. I had never seen anything quite like it. The dressing-room was like a Trinidad Carnival band. Even the senior players were jumping up and down, hugging each other and crying. I was almost overcome with emotion. There was no doubt about it. It had been the great escape. I think what came out of all that emotion was a concerted feeling among the team that we could not afford to lose the competition now. And that carried us through in the end, along with some brilliant cricket.

And so it did. Some of the most brilliant play came from Lloyd himself.

The West Indies had played Australia in the semi-final and had decided that it might be possible to contain their most efficient scorers by keeping the ball well up, straight or just outside offstump. In the team meeting before the final, that had been the dominant topic of conversation. But West Indian tactics on the field were forced to take a back seat when the wily Ian Chappell, just about the toughest competitor in international cricket, put the West Indies in to bat on winning the toss. His decision to bowl first seemed thoroughly vindicated when the first two West Indies wickets fell cheaply. Great hopes had been pinned on Alvin Kallicharran, the diminutive

Guyanese left-hander. But it was not to be his day, and with a mere 50 runs on the board Kallicharran joined Greenidge and Fredericks in the pavilion and the West Indies were in trouble.

Jeffrey Stollmeyer, then President of the West Indies Board, describes how Gubby Allen turned to him and, after Lloyd had played the first few deliveries, said: 'Lloyd looks in good nick today. Watch it, Australia.'

The situation was tailor-made for the big-hitting Lloyd. He was in tremendous form. From his very first boundary to the huge six over deep backward square which took him closer to an unforgettable century, he was in total command of proceedings. The Australians bowled their hearts out, Chappell tried everything he knew, but as Lloyd reached his hundred the Australian captain led the applause. When Lloyd was out caught at the wicket he had made 102 in almost even time, and had left the fighting Aussies a chastened side. The ovation which greeted his return to the pavilion was the most ecstatic Lloyd has ever received. The West Indians in the crowd had savoured every run. They had hailed every boundary with tumultuous acclamation. From 50 for 3 to 199 for 4, when Lloyd departed, the West Indies, inspired by their captain's triumph, marched on to a respectable total of 291. It was never going to be impossible for the Australians to reach such a target, but it was sufficient to make the Australians fight all the way; they were now compelled to throw caution to the winds, to attack from the word go and to take chances, a few of which proved fatal. Scrambling madly for quick singles, batsmen were run out at crucial junctures; Richards alone was responsible for three such dismissals. Adventurous strokes lifted deliveries into the hands of eager West Indian fieldsmen.

The fall of each Australian wicket caused Lord's to explode with the noise of celebrating West Indians, and when Clive Lloyd received the Prudential World Cup trophy from the Duke of Edinburgh all northwest London shook with the ovation. The West Indies captain had also been made the Man of the Match. The game had begun at 11 am on the longest day of the year. Australia were beaten just before nine in the evening. Appropriately, the celebrations continued into the early hours of the morning, when the newspapers confirmed that the West Indies were indeed cricket champions of the world.

One West Indian paper printed this ecstatic review of Lloyd's batting on that day:

Clive set about the Australian attack like a man possessed. In the 36 overs he was at the crease, he made 102 glorious runs – the second 50 coming off only 32 deliveries.

Lord's was alive with the West Indian rhythms; the drums spoke. Lloyd announced his presence at the wicket with a mighty six off Lillee. And he and Kanhai, his childhood hero, took the score from 50 for 3 to 199 for 4 in a classic demonstration of clean hitting from both front and back foot with punishing power.

Denis Compton called it the greatest 60-over match ever played, and to Clive Lloyd he paid this remarkable tribute:

His magnificent 102 was one of the greatest innings I have ever seen. On top of this, he bowled his quota of 12 overs for only 38 runs and took the vital wicket of Doug Walters. As rival captain Ian Chappell said: 'Lloyd's was a magnificent innings which changed the game after we'd got the start I'd hoped for.' The tall majestic Lloyd went like a bomb from the moment he reached the crease. He reached his century off only 82 balls, collecting 12 fours and two sixes in an unforgettable knock brimming with power, grace and elegance.

I can remember only one innings to compare with this one. It was played by the late Stanley McCabe when he made 235 at Trent Bridge in my first Test match against Australia in 1938. Sir Donald Bradman beckoned all his players onto the balcony and said: 'I don't want you to miss this knock. You may never see the like again.'

Well, 37 years later, I can say we have . . . In an incredibly short time, the Australians were reeling, bewildered and finally destroyed by the ferocity of Lloyd's stroke-making. The Australians did not bowl badly. But no one could stop the flow of runs from the maestro's bat. When they bowled only a fraction short, he pulled it with tremendous power to the boundary. When it was slightly overpitched, it was hammered like a rocket through the covers. What an unforgettable knock! What an unforgettable day's cricket!

Lloyd's next big test against the Australians was to be on their own turf and with memories of their World Cup humiliation fresh in their minds. The Australian tour at the end of 1975 marked a significant turning-point in Lloyd's philosophy about Test cricket.

CHAPTER SEVEN
A *New Philosophy Takes Shape*

I try to hit a batsman in the rib-cage when I bowl a
purposeful bouncer and I want it to hurt, so that the
batsman doesn't want to face me any more.

Dennis Lillee

It was the best of times, it was the worst of times.

Dickens

In 1975–76 Clive Lloyd and his world-conquering West Indies side
ran into the pace and hostility of Lillee and Thomson, ably supported
by the talented left-arm swing bowling of Gary Gilmour. Quick
bowling had been no stranger to West Indian players, who revelled in
hooking the short-pitched delivery and who of all international
players seemed to relish the challenge posed by the fast men. But on the
1975–76 tour the Australian quick bowlers had the last word and the
West Indies were sent home to lick their wounds after one of their most
ignominious performances.

Before the start of the first Test, Clive Lloyd wrote: 'There is not
much between the two teams where talents and skills are involved and
you don't need a crystal ball to predict that the outcome could hang on
a slender thread.' That might well have been a sage assessment of the
comparative merits of both sides, especially after the enthralling
World Cup. But not even a crystal ball would have predicted the full
extent of the West Indies humiliation.

In the first Test at Brisbane the West Indies were bundled out for 214
in their first innings. Only Fredericks, who just missed a half-century,
and Deryck Murray, who helped organise a resolute rearguard stand
with a personal contribution of 66, gave any respectability to the West
Indian scoring effort. A marvellous century by Greg Chappell then
took the Australians to a comfortable first-innings lead.

Batting a second time, Rowe and Kallicharran served the West
Indies well. They both got centuries. But Australia's first-innings lead
was 152, and asked to make 219 runs to win the match Greg Chappell,
with another century in his first Test as captain, and his brother Ian put
up an unbroken partnership of 159 to take Australia to a well-
deserved victory with eight wickets to spare.

Far from being discouraged, it looked for everything as though the West Indies had decided to take the battle to the Australians in the second Test at Perth. Australia, thanks mainly to a fine century by Ian Chappell, reached 329 batting first. But then Fredericks first and Lloyd later on cut loose in one of the most devastating exhibitions of strokeplay seen in a Test match. In just over 200 minutes of inspired batting against the ferocity of the Australian pace attack, Fredericks scored 169 runs. Lloyd took over where his fellow-Guyanese left off and smashed one enormous six out of the ground and hit 22 fours in scoring 149. The West Indies raced past Australia's first-innings tally and went on to get 585, 256 runs ahead of their opponents' first-innings total. The Australians were overwhelmed by an inspired spell of fast bowling from Andy Roberts. He claimed the first four Australian wickets and took three more to end the innings with figures of 7 for 54. Beaten out of sight in the first Test, the West Indies won the second by the impressive margin of an innings and 87 runs.

Melbourne was the venue for the third Test match and more than 85,000 people crowded into the ground on Boxing Day to watch the start of the game. The Australians won the toss, but Chappell asked the West Indies to have first strike. And then Dennis Keith Lillee, later to become Australia's leading wicket-taker (overhauling Richie Benaud's 248 wickets during the 1980–81 season), and Jeff Thomson, the Sydney-born 'nature boy', tore into the West Indies batting. Lillee, complete with a Mephistophelean moustache, took four wickets for 56 runs; Thomson, who had once been quoted as saying that if he hit a batsman it didn't worry him too much to see his victim 'rolling around screaming and blood on the pitch', bowled out half the West Indies side at a cost to him of only 62 runs. The West Indies had run into a firestorm and were all out for 224. And out of that Fredericks had made 59 and Richards 41.

The West Indian pace bowlers tried desperately to attack as effectively as their opponents had done. But nothing seemed to go right for them. Catches were dropped and some close umpiring decisions went against them. Gary Cosier, making his Test début, got the benefit of one such close decision and went on to make a hundred. The ever reliable Redpath profited from a chance when he was in the 60s and went on to his century. Then, nearing the end of their innings, Lillee and Thomson, who had destroyed the pride of the West Indian batting, now launched a sustained attack on their bowlers. Thomson was out only six runs short of his fifty, but Marsh, who had also joined in the free-scoring spree, scored 56 and Australia's lead stretched to

261. Facing such a huge deficit, only Lloyd with a resolute 102 stood in the way of the opposition. The West Indies team were demoralised and looked it. They managed to escape defeat by an innings, but could only set Australia a target of 55 runs to win the match. They won comfortably, losing two wickets on the way. It was the beginning of a major West Indian disaster.

The next three Test matches went almost the same way. At Sydney at the start of the New Year, the West Indies were beaten by seven wickets. Rowe, Lloyd, Fredericks and Bernard Julien batted well in the first innings, but Thomson ripped through the batting in the second innings to finish with 6 for 50. At Adelaide, Australia won by the substantial margin of 190 runs and back in Melbourne, towards the end of January 1976, the West Indies were humiliated by 165 runs.

The Australians had bowled well, but there can be no doubt that the West Indies contributed to their own sad demise. The top West Indian batsmen came to be known as the 'Happy Hookers' because of the manner in which they flayed at every short-pitched ball, apparently quite unworried as to the consequences. Viv Richards believes that Australia's win in the first Test so shook the West Indies that they never really recovered, although they did come back with what he calls a 'runaway and deceptive win at Perth'. He says:

> During that first Test match in Brisbane, there seemed to be no order in our dressing-room. No one tried to pull us together. The whole place was in a shambles. And so it went on. Of course, we should have done better, but we gave away our wickets as though we were bent on self-destruction. There was not surprisingly a lot of criticism of our players. Not so much for lack of discipline off the field as lack of temperament on it. We failed too often when the crunch was on.

Gordon Greenidge blames Lloyd for not giving the team the inspiration it needed, although no one was able to accuse him of not carrying his weight with the bat. Lloyd made nearly 800 runs on the tour for an average of 43 and 469 runs in the Test series at just under 47 runs per innings.

Lloyd makes this assessment of that ill-fated tour:

> Our first problem was the obvious fact that in Lillee and Thomson the Australians possessed a pretty deadly attack. None of our batsmen had encountered pace of that quality before. So throughout the series we had only one opening stand of over 50.

That meant our key middle-order batsmen were coming to the wicket with the Australian fast bowlers still fresh and with their tails up. The ball was still new and the bowlers were able to exploit that to advantage. The fact that many of us were hit simply added to the pressure we were under. I was hit on the jaw by Dennis Lillee in Perth and I was hit by Thomson in Sydney. Bernard Julien got his thumb broken and Kallicharran got a painful one on the nose from Lillee in Perth. Every member of the West Indies team at some time or other did feel the pain of a cricket ball being sent down at great speed, thudding into their bodies.

Without wanting to sound as though I'm making excuses for our poor showing, the other point is that we suffered badly from injuries. Holding pulled a muscle in Perth and was out of the third Test, and although we had both Holding and Roberts in the side in Sydney and in Adelaide, Roberts was well below his best and he finally succumbed and missed the final Test in Melbourne. There were even injuries among our support bowlers, Holder, Boyce and Julien.

And then there was the matter of our hooking. Frank Tyson's book on that series was titled *The Hapless Hookers* and someone totted up that we lost some 16 wickets to the hook shot. West Indian batsmen are aggressive and like to fight fire with fire. With the Australians depending so much on fast bowling, a lot of it short-pitched, our batsmen felt that the only way to take the battle to them was to hook and a lot of them perished in the process. I remember discussing the matter repeatedly at team meetings and there was a lot of advice that maybe that stroke should be used with more restraint. But some players insisted that they could not resist the challenge to hook. It was not a particularly professional approach, but in the end I failed to change their minds.

Then there was the question of the umpiring. I fully accept the principle that umpires are in charge of the game, but I also feel it is perfectly natural for Test players to react angrily when they see what they believe is an umpiring error. And there were rather a lot of those on that Australian tour.

In the Melbourne Test match, some decisions astounded us. Redpath, we felt, had been out twice before he reached his century. The first time he was caught behind, the second time at leg-slip. Playing in his first Test, Gary Cosier scored 109, but even before he reached double figures he was trapped leg-before by Julien. An inswinger caught him on the back foot, plumb in front of the middle stump. He couldn't have been more out. And there were at least another half a dozen incidents like those. I have the reputation of being a fairly calm individual but to tell the truth, I had never been more incensed on a cricket field in all my life. Even Lance Gibbs on one occasion snatched his hat from the umpire and instead of giving it back to him when he bowled the next over, stuffed it in his own back pocket.

In the fourth Test in Sydney we all thought Ian Chappell snicked the first ball he got from Holding to Deryck Murray behind the wicket. We appealed but nothing happened. Holding broke down and cried like a child. We had to console him before he was able to bowl again. After that, our morale went to pieces. There was a great deal of debate inside our party about whether we should complain about the umpiring or keep quiet about it. I argued strongly there was no merit in keeping quiet. When I did, it caused quite a stir and one umpire resigned. But it showed we meant business. If an umpire is bad, we say he is bad, just like we say a player is having a bad tour. Why not?

I know that some players blamed me for the collapse of our spirit. Try as much as I could, I was never able to motivate the players on that tour. I couldn't check the downward slide.

But some good did come out of it. Our younger players now knew what it was to be badly beaten. And they were determined never to let it happen again. And I realised how effective it is to have three or four quick bowlers on your side, always keeping the opposing batsmen under pressure. I thought we must do the same as the Australians to succeed. So that even when people kept on at me saying, 'You must play a spinner here or a spinner there', I remembered Australia and how effective that fast bowling combination was.

With that, the new Clive Lloyd philosophy about the use of fast bowlers was born. Back in the seventh century the Greeks initiated the idea of using heavily armed soldiers fighting in closed ranks, known as the phalanx. Lloyd initiated the idea that with four fast bowlers in his team they could all be used as shock troops – as India were to discover later in 1976, when they went to the West Indies. Coincidentally, that series also confirmed Lloyd's doubts about the relative merits of spin bowling.

India's batting on the opening day of the first Test match of the 1976 series in Barbados lost them that first duel with the West Indies. They

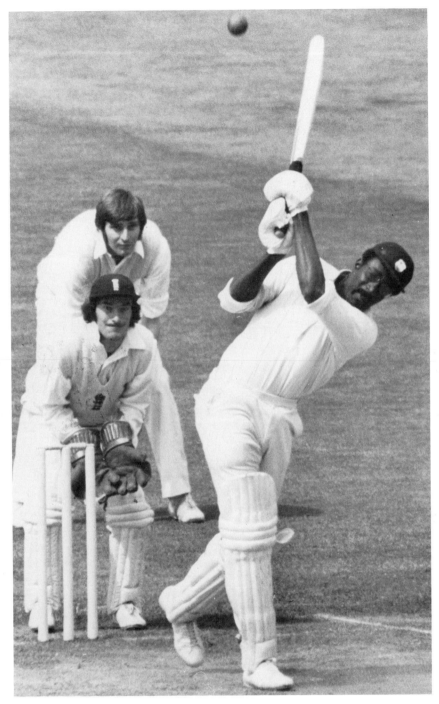

Knott and Old watch as Clive Lloyd hits
out against England.

Clive Lloyd in full flow for Lancashire.
In 1974 (right) he scored 1458 runs at
an average of 63.39.

Above Happier moments of an unhappy tour of Australia in 1975–76: with the Australian captain, Ian Chappell.

Below And with the irrepressible Ian Botham, 1984.

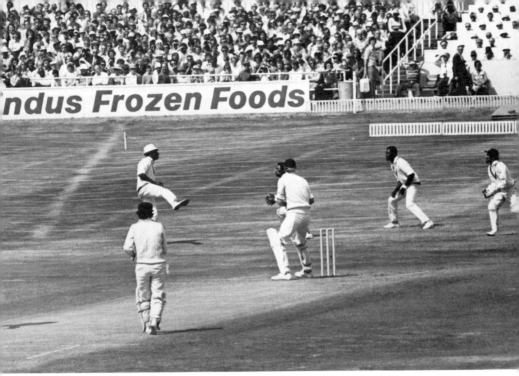

Above The end of Tony Greig's innings of 116 in the Leeds Test, 1976 – caught Lloyd (at third slip), bowled Wayne Daniel.

Below Clive Lloyd hits John Snow for 4 in the first Test in the same series at Trent Bridge. Viv Richards is the non-striker.

West Indian crowds enjoy Lloyd's
aggressive strokeplay against England
(1980).

Another boundary for Lloyd; Alan
Knott is the 'keeper.

Above Lloyd reaches his century against England at the Oval in 1980 with a flourish.

Below Sharing a joke after colliding with umpire Dickie Bird.

were bundled out for a miserly 177, by Roberts, Holding and Julien, with only Madan Lal playing with anything resembling distinction. In reply, the West Indies star batsmen put in a thundering performance. Richards hit a sparkling 142; Lloyd, admirable in support, got 102; Kallicharran fell only seven runs short of his century and Roy Fredericks got 54. The West Indies declared at 488 for 9 and never gave India the slightest chance of getting on even terms. They made 214 in their second turn at the crease and the West Indies had begun the series with a handsome victory by an innings and 97 runs.

There was much more resolution in the Indian batting in the second Test match in Port of Spain, where Gavaskar and Patel both scored hundreds. But so did Viv Richards, who followed up his first Test century at home with another magnificent score of 130. Lloyd made 70 in the West Indies second innings, and with such heavy scoring all round on a perfect Trinidad wicket a draw became inevitable.

Port of Spain was also the venue for the third Test match because Bourda in Guyana had been flooded. The West Indies seemed in no danger at all in the match when the insatiable Richards scored yet another century, this time going on to get 177 superb runs. Clive Lloyd made 68 and Bernard Julien 47, and the West Indies were dismissed for a respectable 359. When Michael Holding ripped the Indian batting apart in their first innings, taking 6 for 65, the match was well and truly in the West Indies pocket. A fine century by Alvin Kallicharran, batting in considerable pain from a shoulder injury, enabled Lloyd to press home his chances of victory. With Kallicharran undefeated on 103, Lloyd declared the West Indies innings closed at 271, leaving India to get just over 400 runs to win the match – a feat which India had never accomplished before. (Only Australia, against England in 1948, had achieved this target. They needed 404 runs in the fourth innings – two runs less than India now required.) The West Indies captain had been persuaded to play three spin bowlers in that Test. The argument ran that the Indian quartet, Bedi, Chandrasekhar, Prasanna and Venkataraghavan, had been turning the ball 'a yard' on a responsive Queen's Park Oval. With India needing 406 runs to win and with a day and one session remaining, the West Indies captain gave the ball to his three spin bowlers, Jumadeen, Padmore and the Trinidadian legspinner Imtiaz Ali. But the trio held no terrors for the consistently masterful Gavaskar and the stylish Viswanath, who both scored centuries and laid the foundations for an incredible Indian victory.

As far as Clive Lloyd was concerned, that was the end of any future 'experiments' with spin bowlers. They had let him down and he has never forgiven them or forgotten that Test match. Back in the West Indies dressing-room he called the three spin bowlers to him and asked with a distinct sarcastic edge to his voice: 'Gentlemen, I gave you 400 runs to bowl at and you failed to bowl out the opposition. How many runs must I give you in future to make sure that you get the wickets?' Nobody ventured a reply. The point had been well taken. Lloyd swore that he would never again be let down by spin bowlers. On wickets fast or slow, he would employ pace. Doing away with spinners would enable him to play four fast bowlers instead of two. His mind had been made up. His distrust of spinners dovetailed neatly with his confidence about the effectiveness of fast bowling.

The fourth and final Test match at Sabina Park in Jamaica turned out to be a most extraordinary affair. Gavaskar accused the West Indies of 'barbarism' and the Indians left for home, looking for all the world like Napoleon's troops on the retreat from Moscow.

India appeared to be on target for a respectable first-innings score. At one stage they were 136 for 1. They had reached 216 for the loss of three wickets when the controversy began. Patel took his eye off a ball from Holder which flew from his bat and hit him painfully on the mouth. Then Gaekwad, tall and a picture of determination, was hit behind the left ear by a delivery which behaved oddly. It flew off a good length and the batsman failed to make good his escape.

Sunil Gavaskar was appalled at what he felt had been blatant intimidation. After the tour he wrote in his book *Sunny Days*:

When I faced Holding, I received four bouncers in an over and a beamer which Holding had pretended had slipped from his hand . . . After one over, I asked the umpire for his definition of intimidatory bowling. To call a crowd 'a crowd' in Jamaica is a misnomer. It should be called a mob. The way they shrieked and howled every time Holding bowled was positively horrible. They encouraged him with shouts of 'Kill him Maan!', 'Hit him Maan!' 'Knock his head off Mike!' All this proved beyond a shadow of a doubt that these people still belong to the jungles and forests instead of a civilised country . . .

The new ball which Lloyd took the next day was just the missile Holding needed for his lethal deliveries. He slipped one out to Mohinder [Amarnath] who was caught by Julien when he deflected a delivery trying to defend his head getting knocked off! The first ball to Viswanath must have been the most frightening delivery he

has ever faced. It almost took his head with it . . . On the dot of
lunch Anshuman Gaekwad, who had taken many blows . . . was hit
just behind the left ear. It was yet another short ball and it went like
a guided missile, knocking Anshuman's spectacles off . . . At this the
crowd were stamping their legs, clapping and jumping for joy.
When Anshuman Gaekwad was forced to retire, the will to fight got
knocked out of us.

Needing a good second-innings score after the West Indies declared
at 366 for 6, India began badly, losing the heavy-scoring Gavaskar for
2. After that only two other batsmen reached double figures and five
Indian players were recorded as 'absent hurt'. This was how India's
second-innings scorecard looked:

S. M. Gavaskar, caught Julien bowled Holding, 2
A. D. Gaekwad, absent hurt, 0
M. Amarnath, stumped Murray bowled Jumadeen, 59
G. R. Viswanath, absent hurt, 0
D. B. Vengsarkar, lbw Jumadeen, 22
B. P. Patel, absent hurt, 0
S. Madan Lal, bowled Holding, 8
S. Venkat, bowled Holding, 0
S. M. H. Kirmani, not out, 0
B. S. Bedi, absent hurt, 0
B. S. Chandrasekhar, absent hurt, 0
Total, 97 for 5.

That was the point at which India's second innings closed, and when
the Indian team took the field with the West Indies needing 13 runs to
win the match the Indian captain Bedi was not among them.
    Lloyd insists that it had not been the policy of his bowlers to harm
the Indian batsmen.

It was never and has never been our deliberate policy to indulge in
unfair tactics. Some Indian batsmen felt that when Holding went
round the wicket to them, he was aiming at their bodies. Quite
simply, it was a ploy to change his direction against batsmen who
were not getting into line and who would then snick the ball to the
wicket-keeper or to the slip cordon. They talked about barbarism
and all that stuff, I can't accept that. There was a spot on the wicket
which made the ball take off. We had quick bowlers and their

batsmen simply couldn't cope. But that's cricket. I can't say I was greatly upset. Because a wicket is quick, and batsmen get into difficulty, you can't bowl half-volleys, you still do your best to get them out. That's the game. If you can't play quick bowling you shouldn't be in the game at international level.

His experiences in Australia facing Lillee and Thomson had made Lloyd uncompromising about fast bowling. The controversy reared its head again a few months later in England.

The tone for the England v West Indies encounter in 1976 had been set by Tony Greig. Appearing on a BBC television sports programme, the new England captain was asked about the prospects for the West Indies tour. In a fashion which was typical of his extravagance, Greig replied that it was the intention of the England team to make the West Indies 'grovel'. It is a comment on his lack of sensitivity that to this day his former colleagues and friends insist that it never occurred to Tony Greig that for a white South African to talk about making a black West Indian team 'grovel' was about the nearest one could come to a formal declaration of the start of World War Three. That was certainly the way Greig's remarks were interpreted by the West Indies. And they resolved to punish him. The team meeting which followed Greig's remarks was more a council of war.

Quite simply [says Lloyd] we were angry. We decided that it was important for us to show Tony Greig and all the other detractors of West Indian cricket that the grovelling days were over. We were in the process of building a side of character and we set out to tell Greig's side just that.

The first two matches were drawn. The most notable feat of the first Test was a giant of an innings by Viv Richards who hammered the England bowling for 232 magnificent runs. The West Indies put up 494 in their first innings. England replied with 332, and although the West Indies declared at 176 for 5 when they batted a second time England were always behind. In the end they hung on for a draw.

The series was to see the maturing of Lloyd's tactics. West Indian commentator and writer Tony Cozier, who reported the series, explains it thus:

Lloyd's tactics were heavily reliant on aggression both from his batsmen and his bowlers, and he used his fast bowlers as shock troops. He had three vastly contrasting physiques and styles but with one vital element in common – real speed: Holding, who had made his Test début in Australia; Andy Roberts, who had already taken 75 wickets in Test cricket; and Wayne Daniel, a heavily-set 21-year-old Barbadian, the least experienced of the lot, accordingly the wildest, but, on occasions, the fastest.

The second Test match at Lord's was an agonisingly close affair and might have produced a result but for the weather. Rain washed out an entire day's play. England batted first and scored 250. But for once the West Indies batting machine failed. Aside from Greenidge's 84 and Lloyd's 50, no other batsmen got among the runs. Richards did not play because of illness. England gained enough of an advantage on first innings to make the West Indies struggle fruitlessly to reach their target in the last innings of the match.

Lloyd's philosophy reached its apotheosis in the third Test at Old Trafford. For the first time, Holding, Roberts and Daniel bowled together in a Test match, and England's weakness against genuine speed was cruelly exposed. However, Mike Selvey threatened to spoil the West Indian party on the very first morning of that Old Trafford Test. He took four wickets in quick succession for 41 runs and only a purposeful performance by Greenidge, who scored a century in both innings of that match, saved the West Indies. Out of a first-innings score of 211, Greenidge's contribution was 134.

But when England batted they faced pace bowling as they never had before. In the end they were just unable to cope. They fell, bedraggled and dispirited, for 71 runs, their lowest-ever total against the West Indies. The wrecker of the England innings was Michael Holding, who went through the England batting like a hot knife through butter, accounting for half the England batting for 17 runs. It was one of the great exhibitions of fast bowling, although the England team didn't appreciate it. Pressing home their advantage, the West Indies piled on the agony when they batted a second time. This time Richards batted fluently to make 135, Greenidge, emulating Headley's feat of 1939, scored his second hundred in the Test, and with more modest but important efforts from Fredericks and Lloyd, England faced the gigantic task of getting 552 runs to win the match. Andy Roberts destroyed any lingering hopes they may have had. He took 6 for 37 as England were dismissed for a sorry 126. The West Indies had won by a massive 425 runs. England were grovelling now. But Lloyd's philosophy had produced results. Roberts took nine wickets in the match, Holding seven and Daniel four.

For a time, Edrich and Close were subjected to a barrage of short-pitched bowling. (This was in the days before helmets.) Bob Willis, who was later to lead England against the West Indies, describes it as the 'most sustained barrage of intimidation' he has ever seen. He adds: 'The umpires did not crack down on it, though it was frightening to watch.'

Clive Lloyd admitted at the time that perhaps the bouncers had been over-used. Their team meeting after the Close/Edrich 'barrage' focused on the merits of keeping the ball well up. 'For the rest of the tour,' says Lloyd, 'we kept the ball up a little more with great results.'

At Headingley, the West Indies won a great Test match by 55 runs. Both sides had fought to the bitter end and only superb spells of hostile fast bowling by Roberts and Daniel tipped the balance in the West Indies favour.

The final Test at the Oval, with the series already decided, was a celebration of West Indian fast bowling. On a lifeless wicket Mike Holding took 14 wickets, to help his side to a victory by 231 runs. Richards emphasised his standing as one of the finest players in the world by scoring 291 runs in the West Indian first-innings total of 687 for 8 declared. Lloyd made 84 in that innings.

At last, the memories of defeat in Australia a year earlier were beginning to recede. And Lloyd believed that he had arrived at the formula which was to dominate West Indian cricket throughout his successful leadership of the side.

For his own part, one remarkable innings on that tour stood out in his mind. It had not been in a Test match but against Glamorgan at Swansea. It was one of those days when everything went right for the West Indian captain. By its end, he had equalled a 73-year-old world record with an unbeaten double century in two hours of sheer batting destruction. He scored 201 in 120 minutes, the time it took the 'Croucher', Gilbert Jessop, to reach his 200 for Gloucestershire against Sussex at Hove in 1903. Of his innings Lloyd said:

> It really was one of my more enjoyable innings. The kind of knock you have when everything is going right. I felt I was in pretty good nick and hadn't really thought about breaking or equalling records . . . but it was nice to know what I had done at the end of a most enjoyable knock.

Enjoyable it might have been for the batting side, but not for the bowlers. Lloyd had gone to the wicket at about 1.20 pm. Returning to the crease after a lunch of chicken salad and tomato soup on a brilliantly warm summer's day, he hit the first of his seven sixes into the holiday traffic along St Helens Road. Twenty minutes later he had reached his first 50 in 44 minutes. Less than ten minutes later, he and Laurence Rowe had put on 100 runs for the fourth wicket. Just after 3 pm he launched a murderous assault on the offspinner Barry Lloyd, taking 25 runs in one over, including one six which went almost 140 yards on its way out of the ground. His 100 came in 80 minutes from only 79 deliveries. He then proceeded to do the incredible even by his own standards. Swinging the bat in a long, almost lazy arc, he reached his double century in 120 minutes from 122 deliveries. It was an exhibition of glorious and savage batting.

One Australian bowler, when asked why he thought Clive Lloyd had never worn a batting helmet for any length of time, ventured the dry comment: 'Lloydie never seems to need one. But when you're bowling to him, it's not a bad idea to wear one yourself.' With Packer's World Series Cricket around the corner, the day of the helmet had almost arrived. But Lloyd was rarely to wear one. He says:

I am not against people using protective helmets to bat. It's better than complaining about fast bowling. If a batsman feels it gives him protection, fine. I have tried them myself. I began to think of it very seriously after I was hit on the chin very painfully by Dennis Lillee in the 1975 series in Australia. But I can't wear the ones with visors; they tend to steam up a little in the heat and blur the vision if you are wearing glasses. But I have occasionally worn helmets without visors on practice pitches which may not be totally reliable.

CHAPTER EIGHT
The Packer Revolution

Men are not made for safe havens.

Aeschylus

For Clive Lloyd and his West Indian side, 1975 and 1976 brought victory in the World Cup, defeat by the Australians 'down under', a morale-boosting, if controversial, victory over India in the West Indies, and a convincing victory over Tony Greig's England team in England.

The year 1977 brought talk of 'revolution', 'the end of the game as we know it', lawsuits and recrimination, and a desperate attempt by the international cricket establishment to assert its right, and its right alone, to administer the game worldwide.

One name rang through the hallowed corridors of world cricket: Kerry Packer, the Australian magnate whose company had given birth to the idea of World Series Cricket. That was the most polite way to which it was ever referred. To an enraged cricket establishment, well supported by the most influential sports columnists of the day, what Packer was planning had nothing to do with cricket at all and would amount to little more than a travelling sideshow, a circus. And that is how it was known. Packer's plan to hire the cream of the world's cricketers and to pay them well to play competitively at various locations throughout Australia came to be called 'the Packer circus'.

From the moment he first heard about World Series Cricket, it was the most natural thing in the world for Clive Lloyd to decide to join the new venture. It offered almost everything West Indian players, more so perhaps than cricketers in other parts of the world, had hoped for.

The careers of West Indian cricketers have always been precarious. Because there is no fulltime professional cricket in the islands, cricketers must come to England to 'make a living' playing the game. At the end of their playing days West Indian cricketers had to keep on trying to find some other form of work, since the financial rewards from cricket had never afforded a comfortable retirement. That fact has always haunted West Indian players, many of whom return to their countries of origin, where employment possibilities have always been at a premium.

So while the cricket establishment saw Packer as an iconoclast, who had bludgeoned his way into the inner sanctum of the sport with the sole intention of tearing the structure to pieces, many players saw his idea as the realisation of a dream, the dream of financial stability in their chosen trade. That is precisely how Clive Lloyd saw it. There was no doubt that it had been vital for Packer to sign up the West Indies captain. But for his part, Lloyd scrupulously left the other players to make up their own minds – though from the moment he himself signed up there was no question that the rest of the West Indies team would follow suit. Lloyd was aware that in deciding to join Packer's scheme he might be putting his captaincy of the West Indies side at risk. That was a real worry. He was enjoying the pressures and stresses of the job; he had by 1977 begun to learn to treat 'those two impostors, triumph and disaster, just the same'. But much more was at stake in joining the Packer World Series plan.

> The principal thing which operated in my mind was the financial security offered by my World Series contract. Here it was; a few months after leading the West Indies to a creditable performance against England, I was being offered three times what I had been paid for that series. Many of us never imagined such sums of money were possible in cricket. Several West Indian players at the end of their careers in the big time either played on in minor leagues to keep going or tried to get coaching jobs with governments and so on. I simply could not see myself doing that when I gave up the captaincy. I was giving my all to cricket; it was not unreasonable to go for something which rewarded people according to their talents. Neither did I feel that I was in any way 'letting down' the West Indies Board. Certain decisions about one's future have to be taken, with a view to doing what is best for a player and his family. [Clive had married in 1971 and shortly afterwards started a family.]
>
> The campaign against Mr Packer was quite outrageous. It just made many of us more determined. Instead of making World Series Cricket weaker, it made it much stronger.

Predictably, Lloyd became one of the lynchpins of Packer's operation to sign the best West Indian players.

> They were hectic days – lots of phone calls from Australia at all hours of the night – and then I met the man himself. I had always wanted to, ever since hearing about what he had proposed. And

when I did, I was terribly impressed. He talked straight, said what he wanted to do, how he thought it could be achieved and the part we were to play in it. It was really everything one had hoped for. He would pay us well, if we delivered our best to his project. We would be well treated too. We were given a tremendous lift by the competent way in which the whole thing had been arranged. In Australia, WSC assisted with passages and accommodation for wives and families. They were particularly happy to help out financially in this regard over Christmas and New Year. Nothing like that had ever happened in all my years of playing cricket for the West Indies. We were bound to be impressed.

The one thing which the critics continually hit upon was the revolutionary aspect of Mr Packer's plans, all the innovations, night cricket and the white ball, new methods of preparing wickets, alterations to certain rules, coloured clothing, etc . . . but in all the critics proved wrong. We had some criticisms about some aspects of the thing; the travelling was exhausting, some fixtures might have been better arranged, but we also felt we had some say in shaping the creation of this new idea. That was new and very pleasant for the players.

The opprobrium of the world of international cricket brought the Packer players closer together, but the competition among them, far from being a cosy circus, was fierce.

The one fact that some people failed to register early on was that here were the best players in the game, playing in competition against each other. We all had something to prove. If you were to stand out in that company, you had to play to the best of your ability. So that there was bound to be good cricket, because it was fiercely competitive. And we knew the world was watching. Many wanted us to fail. We had to do well. The start was shaky. Few people came to the matches, some of the venues had not been previously associated with cricket, but gradually acceptance of the idea took hold and people realised that it was not a hair-brained scheme but a new cricket idea.

When the first World Series season ended, all the West Indian players returned to the Caribbean to play against Australia. Lloyd says that, although the reasons why West Indian players had chosen to play for Packer had been understood by the Board, there was, on the players' return, 'a certain coolness'. When (as described in Chapter One) the break came with the West Indies omitting certain World Series players for the third Test match against Australia and Clive Lloyd resigned in protest, he was sure his grounds were sound.

The whole matter of the clash with the West Indies Board should never have happened. It was avoidable. But I would be tempted to do the same thing again, if the same situation arose. We were told that the players dropped by the selectors were omitted so that other players could be tried with a view to the next series against India. But it simply made no sense. We were playing against the Australians. We were two-up in the series and there was talk of wanting to change the team.

It was an Australian journalist who made me realise something was afoot when he came to my room to do an interview with me just before we met to choose the team for the third Test. He hinted that he had heard that a decision had been taken to make a number of changes to the team which had won the first two Tests. The second hint was that when I suggested to a friend before the meeting that it was likely to be fairly short, one of the selectors disagreed, saying it could be a long one. And as soon as the meeting began, it was clear to me that I was being presented with a plan which had been worked out well beforehand.

I stuck to my point of view, insisting that no player should be dropped if he had done well enough to keep his place. Why change a winning side, I repeatedly asked. Nobody could answer that to my satisfaction. The meeting went on for more than four hours, well into the early hours of the morning. It was no help, all that time spent talking about the subject. In the end, I simply could not put my signature to the team the West Indies selectors decided to play in Guyana. Neither could I lead such a team. So within an hour of the end of the meeting I phoned the selectors to say that I was resigning the captaincy of the West Indies side.

Lloyd issued a comprehensive statement to outline why he had acted as he had done.

I have resigned as captain of the West Indies cricket team because I believe that the time has come for the West Indies Cricket Board of Control to make very clear the principles underlying the selection of the present team and to take whoever is selected as captain into their confidence in terms of the criteria for selection.

I agree completely with the principle of building a young West Indian team that will be available for playing in India, but if that is what is happening I find it difficult to understand the dropping of the young and brilliant Desmond Haynes. On the other hand, in building a young team one needs to ensure that one does not turn one's back entirely on tried and proven content, and in this context the dropping of Deryck Murray, who was so instrumental in our winning the second Test, is incomprehensible, bearing in mind that World Series Cricket players have made themselves available for this tour and may be available for the West Indies tour of India.

However, once the basis of selection is clarified, I am willing to give my fullest support to any West Indies team chosen on clear and known principles. I believe that the present situation can be resolved by dialogue, held in private between the players and the Board, and I myself would be available for such discussions.

Lloyd's statement ended:

It has always been for me the greatest possible honour to represent my country and my region and I look forward to being accorded the honour in the future.

My agreeing to play in World Series Cricket organised by Kerry Packer has not interfered with my resolve to use my skills in the interest of my people in Guyana and in the West Indies whose help and encouragement have made me what I am. I stand ready and available to respond to any requests from any of our players for whatever help and assistance I can give.

The Packer controversy dominated the world of cricket throughout 1978 and 1979. (He had offered the players three times what they were being paid in flat salaries, with incentives to earn more through advertising and special promotions.) Even before the crisis ended, Clive Lloyd was reinstated as West Indies captain with a gracious statement from the President of the West Indies Board, Jeffrey Stoll-meyer, who shook him by the hand and said: 'Let bygones be bygones.'

The West Indies were thus set for the second World Cup competition, to take place in England in 1979. Lloyd's team had been drawn in a group which included New Zealand, Sri Lanka and India, and at

Birmingham on 9 June they beat the Indians easily by nine wickets. Lloyd won the toss and his pace bowlers (Roberts, Holding, Garner and Croft) extracted whatever early moisture there was in the Egdbaston wicket with deadly effect. The first five Indian wickets fell before they had scored 80 and only a superb innings of 75 by Viswanath enabled the team to reach a total of 190. It was clearly not large enough to worry the West Indian batsmen, and with Greenidge getting a hundred, India were left a long way behind, the West Indies scoring the required runs for the loss of only one wicket.

Lloyd's knock of 73 not out was one of the mainstays of the West Indian batting against New Zealand a week later. The West Indies had been sent in to bat by the New Zealand captain, Burgess. Haynes and Richards fell cheaply but Lloyd and Greenidge held the innings together to steer their side to a score of 244 after 60 overs. Roberts, Garner, Holding and Croft kept the New Zealand scoring on a tight rein and they were finally out 32 runs short of their target.

Against Pakistan at the Oval, the West Indies never seemed likely to lose the match when they scored 293 off their 60 overs. The top batsmen all got going; Greenidge made 73, Haynes 65, Richards 42 and Lloyd 37. Majid bowled well for Pakistan, but the big disappointment was Sarfraz Nawaz, who was hit for 71 runs in his twelve overs. When Pakistan replied, Holding made the initial breakthrough, and although Majid Khan and Zaheer Abbas batted brilliantly to put on 166 in 36 overs, no other batsmen shone. Lloyd's most brilliant stroke in the Pakistan innings was the introduction of Viv Richards into the attack. The Antiguan batsman conceded 12 runs in his first over, but then removed Asif Iqbal, Mudassar Nazar and Imran Khan (caught and bowled for 6) and the West Indies romped home with nearly 50 runs to spare.

The Final at Lord's on 23 June 1979 took place in a Caribbean Carnival atmosphere. Mike Brearley, who had the reputation of being one of the shrewdest captains in cricket, won the toss and asked the West Indies to bat first. Lloyd had no quarrel with that tactic. He said of the England decision:

> It may have seemed strange to some people, but many captains are of the view that the wickets in one-day matches tend to get easier and so one sure way to gain an early advantage might be to put the opposition in and capitalise on any early life in the strip and then have the better wicket to bat on and to start the chase for the runs required to win. And, of course, in that World Cup, when we were

four down for 99, it did seem to justify what Mike Brearley had done.

That, though, was the last England really saw of the match. With Greenidge, Haynes, Kallicharran and Lloyd back in the pavilion, Viv Richards and Collis King in indomitable mood took hold and the England bowlers paid a heavy price.

Brearley had a choice [says Lloyd]. Having got four of us cheaply, he had to decide whether to use his 'fill-in' bowlers against the middle order and keep his better strike bowlers for the latter part of the innings or vice versa. He decided to use his 'fill-in' bowlers and Viv and Collis murdered them, effectively putting the match beyond England's reach.

Lord's has seen few innings more inspiring and unrestrained in its attack than Collis King's that day. He mercilessly tore into Gooch, Boycott and Larkins, striking three sixes and ten fours and making 86 of the 139 runs put on for the fifth wicket. England's troubles might have been over were it not for the fact that when King fell, Richards remained. England took the next four West Indies wickets for 48 runs, but with Richards steering the team to respectability the West Indies were never really in as deep a hole again as they were when their first four batsmen had been sent back. Richards, Man of the Match, stayed to the end with an unbeaten 138 – three sixes and eleven fours.

The 287 runs England needed to beat the West Indies were never going to be an easy task, but even so they set about it with exaggerated caution. Lloyd's judgement is brief:

Certainly they needed a good, sound start; but in limited-over cricket you also have to attack, and although Brearley and Boycott put on 100-odd for the first wicket they had consumed too many overs. When that happens the team gets a good start alright, but there's then too much pressure on the other batsmen to force the pace. In trying to do that they take risks and in that kind of cricket that's one of the tactics the bowlers use. Bowlers want batsmen to take undue risks. That's what trapped England really.

Boycott and Brearley put on 129 for the first wicket, but Boycott had been at the wicket for 17 overs before he reached double figures, hardly the stuff of limited-over batting. When he was dropped by

Lloyd at mid-on off a not too difficult chance, it was widely supposed among the aficionados that perhaps this was the West Indian captain's way of making sure that England made slow progress by keeping Boycott at one end.

The suggestion, Lloyd insists, is unfounded. But the point behind it was sufficiently strong to prove England's undoing. When Brearley was out for 64, caught by King off Holding, England needed 158 runs from the last 22 overs. It was never on. Randall made 15, Gooch 32, and that was it. Botham was out for 4, Larkins for nought, and as Garner and Croft swept through the England lower batting like a firestorm, Old, Taylor and Hendrick all failed to score. Garner took five wickets for 4 runs in eleven balls and was twice on a hat-trick.

The successful West Indian defence of the Prudential World Cup provided a stark contrast between the conventions of 'official' and 'Packer' cricket. Lloyd recalls that he had been offered £50 by the West Indies Board as a captaincy bonus when the team went into the World Cup. The figure was later doubled, but it was nevertheless a far, far cry from the way the players were perceived by Kerry Packer in Australia.

Even sweeter than victory over England in the 1979 World Cup was Lloyd's victory over the Australians in Australia in the 1979–80 mini-series. In five previous tours the West Indies had always been on the losing end, and in 1975–76 they had been humiliated. This time, though, they won two of the three Test matches, the third being drawn, and they also won 85% of all the first-class matches they played on the tour. The batsman of the series from the West Indies point of view was Viv Richards, who scored 140 at Brisbane, 96 at Melbourne, and 76 and 74 at Adelaide. But in the World Series Cup, a limited-overs competition, Richards made 9, 153 not out, 62, 85 not out, 88, 23 and 65.

Richards' average for the Test series was an amazing 96.50. But his captain was not far behind, and although he was never in his best form Lloyd's 121 in the final Test was the highlight of the West Indies first-innings score and a major factor in their crushing victory over the Australians in that Test by 408 runs.

Sad it was then that after such a triumph there should have been such controversy surrounding the behaviour of Lloyd's team in the mini-series in New Zealand. Comments about the tour were in general far less charitable than those of the *Wisden* reporter R. T. Brittenden. He said that in New Zealand the West Indians not only lost a Test series against New Zealand for the first time but also 'their reputation for sportsmanship . . . Their main complaint was about the umpiring and in retrospect there is little doubt that if both sides suffered from debatable decisions, more went against the West Indies than against New Zealand. Both Mr Rodriguez, the manager, and the captain, Lloyd, said there should be neutral umpires in Test matches.'

The manager and the captain roundly criticised the standard of umpiring. 'But,' said one reporter of the series, 'Rodriguez went too far. His allegations went beyond the bounds of acceptable comment when he said that the West Indians were "set up" and "there was no way we could win a Test".'

This was the series in which Michael Holding, having had an appeal disallowed, kicked the stumps out of the ground at the batsman's end and when Greenidge showed ill-disguised temper when the West Indies lost the game. Croft, after being no-balled, flicked off the bails as he walked back to his mark and a little later ran so close to the umpire that he actually shouldered him as he ran past. And, says one reporter, 'it was the height of discourtesy when umpire Goodall, wishing on two occasions to speak to Lloyd about Croft's behaviour, had to walk all the way to the West Indian captain, standing deep in the slips. Lloyd took not a step to meet him.'

Lloyd's version of events is different from that of correspondents and others who saw the series:

> There can be no excuse for bad behaviour. But I would strongly say that we have never been bad sportsmen. At the same time, we cannot be expected to say nothing when other people's mistakes become too glaring. If umpires are bad, why should we not say they are. When players are bad, or if a player is having a bad tour, nobody hesitates to say that. We felt we had to say when we felt things were going badly or wrong, to show that we meant business. And some of the things that happened on that tour were quite ridiculous. It was not just the standard of umpiring when lbw decisions and the like were concerned; even in the matter of getting a ball changed. If we asked for a ball to be changed, the umpires said no. If New Zealand made the same request, Mr Walter Hadlee himself, an official of their Board, would come running out with a box of balls to choose from. We felt that was blatantly unfair and we said so. And if players suspect that there is cheating in a match, it's difficult to expect them not to show their own disapproval. I cannot and will not condone bad behaviour on a cricket field. I've always been a sportsman. But after the things Holding and Croft went through, I also had some sympathy for how they felt, although in the

strictest sense what they did could never be right. We formed the view that New Zealand were out to win whatever the cost and that everyone was involved in the effort. It was not a pleasant tour.

The West Indies went home in disgrace, beaten (by one wicket) in the one Test match out of three which reached a conclusion.

In 1980 Clive Lloyd led the West Indies on their eleventh tour of England. Bad weather had the major say on the tour and of the five Test matches only one came to a firm conclusion, the first at Nottingham at the beginning of June, which the West Indies won by two wickets. Helped greatly by Lloyd's batting and the pace bowling of Croft, Garner, Holding, Marshall and Roberts, the West Indies had the better of all the drawn Tests. Lloyd's first-class average of 48.70 was second only to that of the West Indies star batsman, Viv Richards. When the tour ended, the West Indies had lost only one of their eleven Test matches since the disbanding of World Series Cricket.

Shortly after this tour, England – led by Ian Botham – visited the West Indies. Robin Jackman had been banned from playing in Guyana because of his South African connections, and the England team had no alternative but to leave the country. But apart from that cancelled Test match in Guyana, the West Indies won two of the four Tests played and Lloyd's lowest score during the series was 58. Once again, he was second in the averages only to Viv Richards. But it was the bowling that made Lloyd's team as formidable as any England has had to face. Roberts, Holding, Croft and Garner were always there, pegging away, begrudging the England batsmen every run, fighting for every advantage. Holding took 24 wickets and Croft 17. Lloyd employed the tactic he had dreamed of all along: four fast men in harness, never giving the opposing batsmen a moment's respite.

It was in that very season of 1980–81 that Clive Lloyd, in seven matches for Guyana in the Shell Shield, scored 728 runs for an average of 104. It had been his finest season for his country. Lloyd had missed the first game of the Shell Shield and had only arrived for his first innings terribly late after his flight from London to Georgetown had been delayed. He was saved by a drinks interval at the right time, and joining his countryman Alvin Kallicharran with Guyana in deep trouble at 112 for 6, he helped put on 286 runs for the seventh wicket to establish a new record in Shell Shield cricket.

In 1980 Gillette had handed over the sponsorship of their limited-over competition to the National Westminster Bank, and in a ceremony to mark the event Lloyd was named the outstanding Gillette

Cup cricketer in the tournament's 18-year history. It was an acknow-
ledgement, if any were needed, that he had stamped his name indelibly
on the competition. Few people thought of it without remembering at
the same time the glorious knocks of his which had by 1980 helped
Lancashire win the title a record four times.

Only a few weeks before, in a Roses match at Old Trafford, Lloyd
played an innings which he counts among his most enjoyable and
which helped his side to victory. Yorkshire had declared at 265 for 5 in
their second innings, setting Lancashire to make 302 runs in 250
minutes. It was a challenge tailor-made for the West Indian captain.
The Lancashire opener Kennedy had been caught off the bowling of
Chris Old for 13, and although David Lloyd was batting well
Lancashire appeared in serious danger of falling behind the required
run rate when Frank Hayes was stumped off the bowling of Phil
Carrick for 8. When David Lloyd went for a well-made 61, Lancashire
were 125 for 3. But Lloyd excelled himself with a wonderful display,
hitting 15 fours in 110 minutes, reaching 101 and making light work
of Yorkshire's challenge. After the game there had been some argument about whether the Yorkshire captain had been too accommodat-
ing in his declaration. His mistake was rather that he had forgotten
how the entire character of any game of cricket can be changed by
Lloyd in rampant mood.

This is certainly what happened one season later when Lloyd hit an
undefeated century for Lancashire against Middlesex in a limited-over
game at Old Trafford. Middlesex won the toss and reached 218 for 7
off 39 overs. Lancashire were in deep despair at 71 for 4 when Lloyd
entered the scene. The fifth wicket fell at 87, but it seemed to be the cue
for Lloyd to take command. Mike Brearley, that master tactician, then
tried to contain him. He moved his fielders around with his customary
authority and calm. But Lloyd found gaps everywhere with blistering,
unstoppable, unreachable shots. The fielders went back almost to the
boundary ropes and still Lloyd passed them. As one reporter of the
game said: 'He hit everything cleanly. There were no edgy shots. He
looked as sweetly tuned as the finest Stradivarius. Lancashire did not
beat Middlesex. Clive Lloyd did, as single-handed as anything Francis
Chichester or Chay Blyth have done.'

It was appropriate that during that 1981 season Lloyd became one
of only twenty-five batsmen to have scored 10,000 runs for Lancashire
in first-class matches. And he reached the milestone quicker than any
other Lancashire player.

In 1981–82 Clive Lloyd led the West Indies in three Test matches against Australia, winning one and losing one, with one match drawn. And he was second in the batting averages behind Gordon Greenidge in India's 1982–83 tour of the West Indies, when his Test match average was a respectable 67.83 with two centuries.

The West Indies won the first Test match in Jamaica, and Lloyd scored 143 in the second Test in Port of Spain which ended in a draw. In the following match in Guyana, the West Indies captain's contribution was a fine 81 in his side's first-innings score of 479, but the match was spoiled by the weather and ended in a stalemate. The West Indies won the fourth Test in Barbados by ten wickets; the fifth match of the series was drawn, although batsmen on both sides enjoyed themselves: for India Vengsarkar made 94 and Shastri 102, and for the West Indies Greenidge, Haynes and Lloyd all scored centuries.

Clive Lloyd, ageing gracefully but still commanding his place in the West Indian side by sterling performances just when they were needed, looked forward to the 1983 World Cup with undisguised delight. No one knew better than the West Indies captain that it was going to be a tough competition. Nothing could be taken for granted, but the series of one-day matches would give the West Indies, if they won, a hat-trick of victories in what has become one of the most prestigious competitions in the game.

The first sign that the 1983 competition was going to be different came in the very first match the West Indies played. They were conclusively beaten by India. They lost by 34 runs at Old Trafford and the margin would have been much greater had not Roberts and Garner put on 71 runs for the last wicket. This was living dangerously indeed.

In their second match in the competition Lloyd's men prevailed against Australia and in the end won comfortably by 101 runs, but the West Indies had their anxious moments. Batting first in poor light, they lost Greenidge, Haynes, Richards and Lloyd for 78 runs and only reached their score of 252 for 9 thanks to some excellent batting from Bacchus and Gomes.

Australia's innings began like a whirlwind. Their opening batsmen launched a sustained attack on the West Indies pace bowlers and the West Indies looked in trouble. But once the initial breakthrough had been made the lower half of the Australian batting folded meekly. The man chiefly responsible for Australia's demise was Winston Davis, who set a new record in the competition by taking seven wickets for 51 runs. He did have a rather lively and at times unpredictable pitch to assist him, but he tamed the early savagery of the Australian batsmen and gained the upper hand with some intelligent bowling.

Beating Zimbabwe at Worcester, the West Indies journeyed down to London and the Oval, their favourite ground in England, for their second game against the Indians. They won by 66 runs, but there was never any doubt during the course of the game that they were playing a side whose limited-over cricket had improved beyond recognition.

Against Australia at Lord's, the West Indian batting was in full flow. The Australians had made 273 with good scores from Hughes, Hookes and Yallop. But Gordon Greenidge and Viv Richards were a match for anything on that day. They added 124 in 27 overs, hitting three sixes and nine fours before Australia's total was overhauled, leaving Richards undefeated with 95.

Pakistan were no match for the West Indies in the semi-final, and the West Indians beat them easily, but far more significant was the fact that India had put England out of the competition with a convincing display of the most competent cricket. They had kept England's score well within reach, dismissing them for 213, and then got the runs for the loss of only four wickets.

And yet no one expected the Final between India and the West Indies at Lord's to go the way it did.

India's total of 183 seemed to allay early West Indian fears about the outcome of the competition and possibly lulled them into a false sense of security. In reply they seemed overtaken by a strange hubris. Greenidge went for one, Haynes for 13, and when Richards fell for 33, going at the bowling as though he had not a care in the world, the West Indies had dug themselves into a deep hole. Lloyd pulled a muscle and was unable to begin the rescue act which was now so desperately needed, and India romped away triumphantly by 43 runs. The West Indies were stunned. Some players broke down and cried in the dressing-room. The sounds that night around north-west London were not those of joyous West Indian steel bands but the persistent and haunting beat of Indian drums, celebrating a sensational victory.

Lloyd's disappointment could hardly have been greater. He felt that his team had let him down. 'We played appallingly. India fully deserved to win, but we didn't do much to stop them. Ours was a performance of amateurs. We were dreadful.' In an emotional speech at a function to mark the end of the World Cup, Lloyd announced that he was giving up the captaincy. It was a measure of his disappointment and viewed entirely as such.

Persuaded by the Board to stay on as captain, Lloyd took the West Indies to India four months later determined to avenge the indignity suffered with the loss of the World Cup. In India, reminders of how the

West Indies blundered were to be seen everywhere. Unlike the West Indian authorities, the Indian cricket establishment widely advertised the joy and pride they felt at the national team's achievement, and commercial houses followed suit. The streets of Bombay were plastered with signs praising the Indian team and saying how much firms had given to various players.

It brought Lloyd back to pondering the one thing which perhaps more than any other has dominated his thinking as a West Indian player and captain – the failure of the West Indies Board to show its appreciation of its players, its almost contemptuous disregard for the importance of the team's success. Lloyd's argument, which he repeats endlessly, is simple. In the West Indian cricket team the Caribbean region has the best possible ambassador. West Indian cricket has never been better, never more universally recognised as the greatest in the game. Yet the Board shows little sign of communicating its pleasure about such a status to the players.

Nobody [says Lloyd] shows any appreciation really for what we have done for the game and the region. India, after they won the World Cup, opened my eyes. The Indian players were given money, endorsements; some were given luxury flats. What do we have to show for having won two World Cups? Not a great deal. What would we have got if we had won the third? Not much.

There is even a hint of bitterness in Lloyd's words, which bodes ill for the future of West Indies cricket should the Board fail to bridge what is perceived by the players as a gap in understanding and communication, almost a gulf between how the players and the Board think. Having failed to bridge that gap with Lloyd at the helm, the worry must be that the West Indies cricket authorities may never again have such a favourable window of opportunity. Lloyd's occasional strictures against the Board are nothing when compared to the harsh and uncompromising judgements made by players like Andy Roberts, Gordon Greenidge and, more to the point, the heir apparent Viv Richards. How Richards will lead the West Indies is one technical question. Another consideration falls into a more general category. It is how he and the Board will resolve the differences which mark them so much apart. That, in the end, will be the determining factor about the Richards era.

For Clive Lloyd the full tour of India in 1983–84 was sweet revenge. India were comprehensively outplayed; they lost three of the six Test matches – the rest were drawn – and the West Indies won every single one of the one-day internationals. There could have been no more complete reversal of what West Indies had come to regard as the 'aberration' of the 1983 World Cup.

The sweetest part of the victory for Lloyd was his own batting. Approaching the grand old age of 40, he was the best of his team's batsmen by far. He scored centuries in the second and fifth Tests, and his tour average was an incredible 82.6. Not bad for a man thinking of retiring! It was his batting against the Indians which helped persuade the West Indies Board that Lloyd should lead the team against England in 1984 and against Australia later that same year.

Now that he has retired from the captaincy of the West Indies, he is still deeply concerned about the game's future, hoping that the Board does not, like Othello, throw 'a pearl away richer than all his tribe'. Lloyd says:

The Board must show the players they are appreciated. The region must do the same. And we must get our own house in order. We must look to the future of West Indies cricket, to keep it at the high level it is now. It can be done with regional co-operation. There is no reason in the West Indies why we should not be thinking again of a common currency, one flag and joint assistance in the promotion of our cricket team.

The days for that may have gone in the strictest political sense. But Lloyd's call for a more regional approach to many of the problems in the Caribbean area may find a more responsive echo in the future.

CHAPTER NINE
England Humiliated

For years, the cheerful reverence accorded successive West Indian teams by Britons at large has been a painful joke to those inside the game.

Robin Marlar

People love watching our fast bowlers.

Jackie Hendricks

If you can't cope, you shouldn't be in the game.

Clive Lloyd

Before a single ball was bowled on his last tour of England as West Indies captain, Clive Lloyd faced a campaign in parts of the English press to discredit not only the 1984 West Indies team but what was perceived as the new West Indies approach to cricket.

As always, the point at issue was the West Indies' dependence on fast bowling. Some commentators could not quite make up their minds whether Garner, Holding, Marshall and Baptiste would 'prove to be a patch on their predecessors', but just in case they were, the sports pages were full of ominous predictions about 'what is unwelcome from the West Indies' and about 'killing cricket the fast way'.

Writing in the *Sunday Times*, Robin Marlar averred that 'Calypso cricket died in the 1950s. Yet such is the public relations instinct of leading figures in West Indian cricket that this identity they cultivate seems likely to last for ever.'

And when, at a lunch given for the West Indies in the River Room at the Savoy Hotel, Clive Lloyd expressed the hope that the British media would have better things to write about during the summer than 'a bumper war', Marlar concluded: 'Lloyd may feel sensitive about the issue of bumpers. He was skipper when the West Indies barrage was loosed off at Edrich and Close, two brave veterans called back to cope with it at Old Trafford in 1976, when the light was black as pitch.'

Even before a ball was bowled in the series, the conclusion among many sports commentators was that most people upon whose support English cricket depends believe that monotonous fast bowling is both 'brutalising the game and boring to watch'.

There was another, much more serious, point at issue. Unlike those in other countries, the West Indian cricket authorities had, in their bargaining with the England Test and County Cricket Board, refused to accept a minimum number of overs to be bowled during a day's play. This laid the West Indies open to the charge that they would never give their opponents sufficient strike in any day's play to make a significant impact on the course of the game. In other words, the West Indies were being unfair to their opponents.

Clive Lloyd's response to these criticisms is a crystallisation of the views formed over many years in the game, both as player and as captain, and a synthesis of what he believes have been the lessons of the most significant incidents in his career. No attempt to understand the philosophy he brought to the leadership of the West Indies is profitable without an appreciation of these.

Lloyd learnt very early on that cricket at Test match level is unrelentingly tough and uncompromising. And he formed the view that, to be successful, there was no other way in which the game can be played. Writing four years ago about the MCC's 1968 tour of the Caribbean, he had this to say about England's brave and, as it turned out, successful attempt to save the final Test match in Guyana and to maintain their one-nil advantage in the series:

> Cowdrey and Knott fought back, and full credit to them for a partnership of 127 which held us at bay. Throughout England's second innings, however, there were blatant time-wasting tactics. Cowdrey actually ran into the pavilion to change a pad, taking up five valuable minutes. He called for a glass of water to be brought on to the field and, at one stage, waited until the crowd noise subsided, accounting for more valuable time. And to think that he had gained the captaincy after Brian Close was sacked for time-wasting in a county match the previous summer! . . . It was throughout that series, too, that I realised that most Test players were not inclined to 'walk' even though it was clear they were out. Kanhai did in the first Test when Cowdrey caught him low down at slip and indicated he had taken the ball cleanly, but there was none of it from the other side. Until then I had always been under the mistaken impression that cricket was a 'gentleman's game', and that 'walking' was part of its great tradition. However, when I watched players who had been gods to me in my youth stand there and await an umpire's verdict when they hit the ball hard, my mind and my attitude changed.

It is important to remember the point in his career at which Lloyd's 'mind and attitude changed'. It was his first encounter with an England team.

The other seminal experience in Lloyd's career was the roasting the West Indies suffered at the hands of the Australian fast bowlers during the 1975–76 tour 'down under'. Rightly or wrongly, Clive Lloyd formed the view that fast bowling is the most effective way of blasting your opponent off the cricket field. Lillee and Thomson were not the sole reasons for the West Indies' unhappy demise during that tour. The Australians batted better than Lloyd's team and held more of their chances, but the role of the Australian pace attack and its consequences for the West Indies' overall showing in the series was the thing which stood out most clearly in Lloyd's mind.

He says:

We had a whole lot of problems, but the main one was that our openers didn't perform well and our key middle-order batsmen were frequently exposed to Lillee and Thomson, still fresh and still raring to have a go with a relatively new ball. Our players all round were put under constant pressure by sheer pace on some very quick wickets. And many of us were hit. I had a double dose. I got hit on the jaw by Lillee in Perth and by Thomson in Sydney. Julien's thumb was broken, just when we felt he might help solve the problem about our opening batsmen; Kallicharran's nose was cracked by Lillee in Perth and everyone at some stage during the tour felt the discomfort and the pain of being hit by a cricket ball being sent down at more than ninety miles an hour. But that's the game. It's tough. There's no rule against bowling fast. Batsmen must cope to survive.

It would be ludicrously inaccurate to suggest that before that encounter with Lillee and Thomson the West Indies had forsworn the use of fast, or short-pitched, bowling, but Australia in 1975–76 marked the point of Lloyd's Damascus conversion. Herbert Sutcliffe was fond of saying of fast bowling: 'There's some that can play it and some that can't. But them that says they like it, is telling lies.'

After that Australian tour Clive Lloyd became firmly convinced that the best way to win Test matches is to give the opposing batsmen a constant diet of what they don't like. The former England player, Bob Willis, agrees about the effect that Australian tour had on Lloyd's outlook. Willis says in his book *The Cricket Revolution*:

The West Indies tour of Australia in 1975–76 was the tactical watershed for Lloyd's team. They arrived there as World Cup holders, with morale high and a determination to see off Lillee and Thomson with far more aggressive methods than stodgy old England had shown the previous year. Only one Test went beyond the fourth day and the West Indies were slaughtered 5–1. They simply fell apart; they allowed controversial umpiring decisions to upset them; the Australians' occasionally abusive tactics on the field distracted them; and Lillee and Thomson took over 50 wickets . . . Judging by past West Indies selectorial panics, Clive Lloyd seemed lucky to keep the captaincy after that tour. He had learned a few lessons from it. In that series, the West Indies bowled more balls per hour than the Australians – on average they sent down 93 balls per hour . . . It rebounded in their face because it gave the Aussies more balls to hit against demoralised West Indian fielders.

If he had any doubts about the wisdom of that new-found philosophy, they were dispelled totally a few months later when India overhauled a West Indies target of 406 to win a Test match at the Queen's Park Oval in Port of Spain. Spin bowling had let Lloyd down. He had been forced to rely on it and it had failed him. Never again would he be placed in such a position.

It is frequently asserted that the West Indies tend to produce more quick bowlers than spinners. That is not necessarily so, as a look at performances in the domestic Shell Shield tournaments would prove. But after India's victory at Port of Spain in April 1976, the chances of another Lloyd team including three spin bowlers sank forever.

When the controversy started again about the West Indian dependence on fast bowlers during Lloyd's last tour of England, the man himself never paid it the slightest attention. Nearing the end of his international career, he had made up his mind. No amount of criticism in the English sporting press about the monotony of an over-dependence on fast bowling by the West Indies would have made the slightest difference to his thinking. He never gave it a second thought. The criticisms were, as West Indians are fond of saying, like water off a duck's back.

His standard comment was: 'Fast bowling is a part of cricket. And nobody is going to change that now. And people can't start complaining when people bowl fast; that is not cricket.'

Lloyd's view is of course hotly contested and by none more so than some opposing captains. One of Lloyd's sternest critics is the former England fast bowler and captain, Bob Willis. By his own admission, Willis never got on really well with the West Indians he confronted in the Test arena. Willis writes in his book, *The Cricket Revolution*:

Despite the high quality on display, Tests against the West Indies were not pleasant affairs in my time. I sensed an undercurrent of bad feeling on the field of play and afterwards there was little social fraternising between England and the West Indies. The lack of social functions did not distress me too much, but I was more concerned that the colour issue probably clouded relationships.

The feelings appear to have been mutual. Many West Indian players couldn't wait to see Willis lose the England captaincy. Even the usually generous Lloyd was heard to remark: 'We can't wait to see that . . . Willis go. It would be such a pleasant change when Gower becomes captain. Then, win or lose, we could at least have a gentlemanly relationship.'

But Willis says about the West Indian emphasis on fast bowling under the Lloyd captaincy:

Test cricket the West Indian way had become an easy game to play by the end of the seventies – provided you had the means at your disposal. Clive Lloyd had them in abundance: a succession of fast-scoring batsmen who would give him enough time to bowl out the opposition twice, plus a production line of fast bowlers who monopolise the West Indies out-cricket. Running their team in the field as regimented as crop rotation, Lloyd would perm four fast bowlers from an impressive selection and simply wheel them up at selected stages.

The batsman Sunil Gavaskar, recently recalled to the Indian captaincy, is no less forthright in his criticism of Lloyd's emphasis on the use of quick bowlers.

Barbarism is what happened on our 1976 tour in the West Indies. The West Indies fast bowlers were determined to either get us out or send us to hospital. The captain, Lloyd, seemed desperate, fearing his future was at stake.

Lloyd's response to all this is simple. He insists that fast bowling is a part of the game and that there can be no logical condemnation of the art when it is done well. He would point out that fast bowlers have always regarded themselves as providing their captain with a sharp weapon against the opposition.

As Frank Tyson wrote in his autobiography:

> To bowl quick is to revel in the glad animal action; to thrill in physical prowess and to enjoy a certain sneaking feeling of superiority over other mortals who play the game. No batsman likes quick bowling and this knowledge gives one a sense of omnipotence.

Clive Lloyd could hardly put it better. And he would not find issue with Harold Larwood, who said:

> The speed bowler must drop a few short. In doing so he puts dynamite into cricket. Every fast bowler in history has done that. And when he does drop one short everybody knows the ball is intended to intimidate, to unsettle, to test the batsman's combination of skill and nerve. When the fast bowler is no longer permitted to make a ball rear at the batsman, cricket can no longer be regarded as a manly game.

During the 1984 West Indies tour of England, some commentators claimed that the short bowling had been overdone. After being dismissed in one innings, the England and Lancashire player, Graeme Fowler, returned to the dressing-room, peeled off his gloves, unbuttoned his pads and was heard to remark that 'the stumps never came into play at all'. It was a *cri de coeur* against what he saw as too many short-pitched deliveries.

Lloyd is uncompromising:

> Short-pitched bowling is part of the quickie's equipment. He can't be too regulated, or he would lose the surprise element. The umpire can't tell a fast bowler that there should be only one short ball an over, because after that the surprise element is lost. Complaints come from batsmen ill-equipped to play the stuff.

Unrepentant though he is about the West Indies tactic of using four quick bowlers, Clive Lloyd does attempt to deal seriously with the question of over-rates. The persistent charge against his team has been that by using four pace bowlers the West Indies consistently limit the opportunities opposition batsmen have or are given for scoring runs. If batsmen face only 11 overs an hour, as against 15, their chances of getting a good score are proportionately lessened.

Lloyd can understand the general argument but fails to follow it through. And he puts the proposition differently, from the point of view of the bowling side:

If you have to bowl so many overs in a day, certain kinds of thinking on the part of the batsmen are inevitable. An opener will be very well aware that with two quick bowlers operating, the time must soon arrive, because of the necessity to get a required number of overs in that day's play, the time will soon come when the captain, to increase the tempo, must employ a spinner or a medium-pace bowler.

A sensible opening batsman, who was finding it difficult to get the quickies away, could bide his time and get his runs off the slower men. By the time the quick bowlers returned, the opening pair could be well dug in. Facing the quickies again, when you've got a few runs on the board, or a hundred partnership say, is a very different proposition from facing them when you've just come in, still desperately trying to get a few. That's the argument against this business of over-rates. In any case, though, it's made difficult if you can't tell a side how many fast bowlers to choose. I am not sure that if every side had four fast bowlers of the quality that we have, they wouldn't choose them or they'd leave them out because of what somebody says about over-rates. If England or Australia or India had Marshall, Holding, Garner and Baptiste, you think they'll decide to drop one or two of them? I don't believe they will. And that is why some of us feel that people only complain when they are at the receiving end. If they were dishing out the medicine, they wouldn't be talking about over-rates and so on. A lot of nonsense is talked also about fast bowling killing cricket. How is it killing cricket? The team which has been consistently the most popular and the most successful in terms of gate money, advance receipts and all that has been the West Indies and we have always had fast bowlers. I haven't heard anyone saying: 'I am not going to see the West Indies team because they have too many quick bowlers.' Interestingly enough, the England players don't complain either. So I'm not sure who is making the criticism or for what purpose.

We have fast bowlers who get people out. That's what the game is all about, and there's no reason why we should change because we keep beating teams.

In full flow on the question of fast bowling and the West Indies team, Lloyd switches the emphasis to the question of short-pitched bowling:

In one of the Tests, Dickie Bird said he thought we were bowling too many bumpers. He said we should bowl two an over at most. That's not acceptable. It's ridiculous. The short-pitched ball is the bowler's surprise weapon. If he is restricted to one an over, once he has bowled that ball the batsman knows that's it, he doesn't have to worry anymore. The bowler's capacity to surprise the batsman is lost. Bird said something like 'space the bouncers out'. I don't know what that means. A lot of these things wouldn't be said if batsmen could handle the pace. They bowl bouncers to us. We hook them for four, or our batters get out trying the hook shot. We don't complain. They can't handle pace. That's why they complain. In the series just gone, there was also one occasion when a nightwatchman had been sent in and batted at number three. Pat Pocock at the Oval. Now what is a bowler to do, feed him half-volleys because he's not a recognised batsman, although he's in at number three? No. At that stage of an innings, you have to try to get people out. If he can't play, he should not be sent in there.

Those were the more controversial elements in an historic West Indies tour of England, a tour during which, for the first time ever, the West Indies completed an unprecedented rout of their opponents. They won every one of the five Test matches played and by embarrassingly large margins. On every occasion when England appeared to 'get into' a match, they were steamrollered by the tourists.

It hadn't taken long for shrewd observers to realise what a gloomy fate awaited David Gower's England team. After the first Cornhill Test of the summer the *Sunday Express* headline read: 'West Indies make it a shambles', and then in bold type pronounced apocalyptically: 'WE'RE DEAD AND BURIED'. For good measure the writer and former England batsman, Denis Compton, added: 'What a battering for our cricketers. I cannot remember ever seeing an England side so utterly humiliated, as the West Indians took our bowlers by the scruff of the neck . . . The irritating thing was that at times they seemed to be toying with us.'

That was in mid-June. The massacre, or what exuberant West Indians called 'the blackwash', had begun two weeks earlier. The executioner in the first of the three one-day internationals was Vivian

Richards. In the words of the cricket correspondent of *The Times*, 'just as Bradman used to do, Richards spoilt the game'.

After the first 26 of their allotted 55 overs, the West Indies were in trouble at 102 for 7. The first wicket had fallen before the score reached double figures, and five wickets, including Lloyd's, were down with the score at 89. But Richards, as devastating as he has ever been, launched a sustained and memorable assault on the England bowling. Receiving 170 balls, he struck 21 fours and five sixes, and in three hours and forty minutes made the highest-ever score in a one-day international, 189 not out. Richards hit five sixes after reaching his century; one, a straight drive off Pringle, went clean out of the ground at the City End. His most incredible shot was his favourite cover-drive off the bowling of Foster. This one, though, was executed from a couple of feet outside the leg-stump and, in the words of one spectator, 'turned the England fielders into stone'.

The Richards' onslaught bled any resistance England might have had left. Chasing a score of 272, they folded meekly for 168, Garner taking 3 for 18 and Richards chipping in with two wickets in his eleven overs for 45 runs.

To the surprise of most people, England won the second of the one-day internationals at Trent Bridge by three wickets. The West Indies again batted first, recovering from 75 for 5 to reach 179 all out, thanks mainly to an innings by Clive Lloyd. Taking the West Indian side under his wing, Lloyd jumped out and drove Miller for a huge six, after being let off at slip, and from that moment always looked a picture of calm resolution. He elegantly square-drove Pringle and hooked Botham over deep backward square. When he was caught by Pringle off Miller, he had made 52 and was his side's top scorer.

England began well, but were then made to scramble disconcertingly in the final stages of their chase. But they achieved their target having lost only seven wickets and with a shade over seven overs to spare. The West Indies had no excuses for their showing. Lloyd repeated his view that the outcome of the series was not as clear-cut as had been predicted, and that England's victory in the second one-day match proved his point.

But at their team meeting before the final one-day international, the West Indies concentrated on doing much better. Much of the strategy and planning was devoted to that. The captain had a few tough words for an apparent slackening-off in effort by the team and everyone arrived at Lord's determined to take on England with a renewed spirit of aggression. Although Clive Lloyd, always the diplomat, refrained from saying unkind things about the England team, no one in the West Indies camp seriously doubted the team's ability to crucify England. But application was what was needed. Because the West Indies had been beaten so rarely in the past two years there had been a tendency not to take every match seriously. In the second one-day international at Trent Bridge the West Indies had never seriously got down to business. And they had discovered to their cost what a dangerous anodyne immunity from defeat can be.

At Lord's on Tuesday, 4 June, a capacity crowd watched Lloyd put England in. The England opening pair put on 60 before they were separated, but after that wickets fell at a fairly regular rate. David Gower, who had been named England captain for all five Test matches before the game, made 29 and Ian Botham 22. But there was little fight in the other England batsmen. 196 was all they could collectively muster.

When the West Indies replied, Haynes and Greenidge put on 50 for the first wicket, and when they went Gomes and Richards took complete control, guiding the West Indies to safety with nine overs to spare. The great Richards was left undefeated with another dazzling innings of 84 not out, including a beautifully struck six off Bob Willis. That six was part of his first 25 runs, which also included four fours.

England had not been disgraced, but Gower must have known that his work would be cut out if he was to beat the West Indies over five days. By the end of the third day in the first Test at Edgbaston, the new England captain could only hope for rain to save his team. 'We are clearly not going to win,' he asserted with refreshing candour. 'All we can hope for is something to happen, probably rain.'

Gower had won the toss and surprisingly chose to bat. Almost immediately, Fowler was caught down the legside off a glove in front of his ribs, and then Randall, being brutally sacrificed at number three, played a snarling lifter from Garner down onto his stumps. And then tragedy. Newcomer Andy Lloyd seemed to be working out his own method of coping with the West Indies attack when he lost sight of a ball from Marshall, which did not get up as steeply as he had anticipated, lowered his head a few inches and ducked right into the ball. It hit him on the right temple guard of his helmet. He looked terribly ill for a while, but was able to walk unaided to the pavilion and spent eight days in hospital under observation.

This renewed the controversy about intimidatory bowling, which arose later in the game when the umpire warned Marshall for

Clive Lloyd acknowledges the applause
of the crowd at Sabina Park, Kingston,
Jamaica, in April 1984, after receiving a
silver salver to mark his 100th Test
appearance.

Three of the fast bowlers who caused England's batsmen so much pain in 1984: *Above left* 'Big Bird' Joel Garner – so often almost unplayable; *Above right* Michael Holding, still a lethal force; *Right and Below* the fastest and most dangerous of them all, Malcolm Marshall.

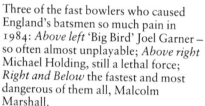

Above Derek Randall is caught by Lloyd off Garner in the first Test at Edgbaston in 1984.

Below Fitness has become one of the most important aspects of the West Indies game. Here the team warms up at Lord's in May 1984.

Above Umpire Dickie Bird warns Clive Lloyd about too many short-pitched deliveries from Malcolm Marshall.

Below Lloyd congratulates his Lancashire colleague Graeme Fowler on his century in the second Test against the West Indies at Lord's in 1984.

Opposite The captain applauds one of his many protégés: Larry Gomes, out for 143 in the first Test at Edgbaston.

Above With Dujon and Richards on the way to a historic 5–0 victory over England in 1984.

Below The verdict of the fans after the West Indies completed their rout of England at the Oval.

Above Clive Lloyd with his heir-apparent, Viv Richards. The West Indies Board may find dealing with Richards a different proposition.

Below A morning's work well done: Harper, Garner, Lloyd and Richards on their way to lunch in the one-day international at Lord's in 1984.

Above The Lloyd children celebrate their father's honorary degree from Manchester University, early 1984.

Below Clive Lloyd, with his wife Waveney and West Indian UN representatives, after addressing the UN on apartheid and sport.

intimidation. The Editor of *Wisden Cricket Monthly*, David Frith, wrote:

It has long been accepted, with resignation, that very few fast bowlers or their captains are prepared to exercise 'reasonable' control over the short pitcher. This profoundest of responsibilities, with its moral tailback, is brushed away, to be picked up by the umpire. West Indies skipper Clive Lloyd's tossing away of the ball after an official warning was most disappointing.

Lloyd's response:

I could not agree with umpire Bird. Nor did he seem to be too clear about what he wanted us to do. Botham was at the wicket. He seemed quite prepared to take up the challenge, yet the umpire was warning us. I do not think that at that point there was any question of our overusing the short-pitched delivery.

Gower, coming in at number four, stayed for just over an hour, never looked entirely happy, and departed caught off the bowling of Holding for 10. When Lamb went for 15, caught in the slips by Lloyd off Baptiste, England were 89 for 5 and reeling. They never recovered. Botham's duel with the West Indies pace attackers brought him 64 well-made runs, but he had never been allowed to assume total command. England were all out for a paltry 191.

The West Indies began badly. Willis, who had earlier announced his imminent retirement from Test cricket, trapped both Greenidge and Haynes leg-before before the score had reached 50. But then Gomes and Richards took over, adding 206 runs and putting the West Indies well on the way to a commanding first-innings lead before they were separated. Gomes' 143 was his highest-ever Test score and his first Test century against England.

In just under three and a half hours Viv Richards had scored 117, his seventeenth Test century, seventh against England and fifth in England. Only Sir Donald Bradman, who scored eleven centuries in England, and Gary Sobers, who scored five, have had such a record against England at home. During the course of his innings Richards passed 5,000 runs in Test cricket.

But England's agony was only just beginning. Clive Lloyd strode to the wicket and before he was out caught by Pringle off Botham, the West Indies had passed 400. Lloyd's contribution was 71, taking him above Sir Len Hutton and into seventh place in the number of runs scored in Tests of all time. His tally of 6,975 runs was exceeded at the time only by Gavaskar 8,394 (later to increase), Boycott 8,114, Cowdrey 7,624, Hammond 7,249, Greg Chappell 7,110 and Bradman 6,996. Lloyd was to move up higher in the table by the end of the series.

And still the West Indian runs came. This is Denis Compton's account in the *Sunday Express*:

> Every home supporter must have cringed at the sight of the tail-enders, Holding and Baptiste, thrashing the England attack in a record-breaking ninth-wicket stand of 150. Holding, in the side for his fast bowling, slammed four enormous sixes and eight fours in his brilliant 69 and Baptiste hit another 11 fours in an unbeaten 87.

By the time Holding and Garner were out in one Pringle over, the West Indies had taken a stranglehold on the first Test with a massive lead on first-innings of 415. The match at that stage was exactly half-way through its scheduled five days.

England got off to the worst start imaginable. Fowler, Randall and Gower were all sent back by Garner in an inspirational spell of fast bowling by the time the score had reached 37. By stumps on Saturday, England were 112 for 4 and the end was only a matter of time. There were few people at Edgbaston on Monday to see the unhappy final rites pronounced over England's demise. Botham had his duel with Holding and Marshall and umpire Dickie Bird intervened. It all seemed academic. Willis hit Harper for 18 runs in one over and reached 22 before he fell to Garner, but the West Indies steamrollered their way to victory by an innings and 180 runs, England's fourth heaviest defeat ever and their first at the hands of the West Indies at Edgbaston.

On the eve of the Test Clive Lloyd had stood in the bar of the team's hotel contemplating the prospects for the match. He had been surrounded by a group of West Indian wellwishers, who were all very confident that England would have no possible chance of beating the West Indies. Lloyd listened quietly to the praise being heaped on his team, occasionally nodding in agreement, but he was incredibly modest about his team's chances. 'We've got to play as well as I think we can. But all cricket matches are difficult. You can't let the other side get away from you. That's why at tonight's team meeting we talked about keeping things tight.' He paused, looked around, announced he was going off to get an early night's rest and added as he left: 'I'd love to leave Edgbaston one up in the series.'

The West Indies did. And from that point on there was no catching them. It was the team's 29th victory in 65 Tests under Lloyd's captaincy. It had taken their unbeaten sequence to 19 and it was their sixth consecutive Test in which they failed to lose a single second-innings wicket.

Clive Lloyd was about to bow out of Test cricket in England in the most memorable and distinguished way possible. He was about to do better than any West Indian captain had ever done in the history of the game, and better against England than any other country had done against England at home.

CHAPTER TEN
The Apotheosis of Speed

We do suggest that we should all face the facts. The
first is that the West Indies are indeed the best thing
on the pitch anywhere in the world at the moment
. . . If you want entertainment, watch the powerful
West Indies.

The Times editorial after
the Edgbaston Test, 1984

Out of this World, Lloyd.

Sunday newspaper headline

England's humiliation in the first Test at Edgbaston was no match for
the profound despair with which their performance had been viewed
in the country at large. So great was the national trauma that,
sandwiched between leading articles about 'NATO's Radical Change'
and the Government's trade union Bill reaching the House of Lords,
was an editorial in *The Times* entitled 'Scraping the Barrel'. On the
subject of England's showing at Edgbaston it said: 'Floored, humbled,
humiliated, massacred, swamped, slaughtered, battered, pole-axed,
tortured, mauled, buried. Not the Government after the Portsmouth
South by-election, but England . . . after Edgbaston . . . The performance was awful, shameful, grisly, inept, puny. Mighty England
reached a new nadir.' And, as if to poke a little fun at its own expense,
The Times reminded its readers that the summer is the season of
sporting hyperbole.

But the paper did go on to acknowledge what had been suspected
for some time and what the first Test match in Birmingham had only
confirmed – that the West Indies under Clive Lloyd 'were the best
thing on the pitch anywhere in the world' at the time.

If Lloyd believed that too, he was not showing it. He kept on saying
that perhaps the margin of victory in the first Test had given an
exaggerated perspective of the differences between the two sides. He
insisted that it was impossible for a cricket team simply to rely on its
residual strength. It only counted when the team did well on the field.
And so through the summer of 1984 he continually willed his players
to do better. He never ceased to look ahead to even greater, more

sterling deeds. So to the accompaniment of newspaper headlines like the one in a Sunday newspaper which read simply: 'Out of this World, Lloyd', the West Indies went on to Lord's for the second Cornhill Test.

The England captain, David Gower, discerned some small advantage in the belief that after England's defeat in the first Test the England players would have a finer appreciation of the tremendous task they faced and of just what was required of them. But even so, Gower could hardly have been unaware of the quality of the team he was up against. In the four Tests they had played in 1984 before going on to Lord's in June, the West Indies had won two by an innings and the other two by ten wickets, three of those being against the Australians.

Batting first, Graeme Fowler and Chris Broad gave their side a confident start. At one stage Broad, making his Test début, took five boundaries off twelve balls as the line and length of the West Indian fast bowlers strayed. Lloyd's succinct assessment of his bowlers' performance at lunch on that first day was: 'I keep telling them, we must bowl straight.'

Broad went caught behind off the indefatigable Marshall for a well-played 55, and England were 101 for 1. With very few exceptions after that any character the innings may have been given by the opening stand disappeared in disgust. Gower was trapped leg-before by Marshall – the delivery seemed too quick for him – and Lamb and Gatting exited by the same route. Botham was as truculent as he always is even when staring at disaster, and Paul Downton proved a model of responsible, defensive application. Only Fowler, who made 106, stood his ground for long. Having begun so well, England tottered to a first-innings score of 286. Marshall's six wickets for 85 runs was his best bowling performance against England. And yet they weren't out of the reckoning yet – especially when the first three West Indian wickets, those of Greenidge, Haynes and Gomes, fell before the total had reached 50. It was at this point that Viv Richards was joined by Clive Lloyd. Lloyd was more than an example to his younger players. No longer the swashbuckling strokemaker of those former glorious years, he was now the image of West Indian determination not to be left too far behind on first innings. By his own incredibly lofty standards Richards struggled a little, almost as though he were being made to think about his shots, thanks to an inspired spell of outswing bowling by Ian Botham. It was an absorbing battle. The two West Indian batsmen had added 103 when Botham, almost stifling his appeal after hitting Richards on the pad with a big inswinger, saw that umpire Barrie Meyer had lifted his finger, sending the Antiguan on his way. Richards shrugged his shoulders, and later received the satisfaction of an apology from Meyer, who admitted that he had erred. It was a gesture of which only the biggest men are capable.

Lloyd's useful, watchful knock ended when he too was trapped in front by Botham, bowling his heart out like the genius of swing he can sometimes be. Lloyd had made 39 and in doing so passed 7,000 runs in Test cricket. The West Indies, still short of 200 and a long way from overhauling England's first total, were given able assistance by their bowlers. Marshall, the scourge of the England batting only the day before, carved his way to 29 and Baptiste did even better, getting 44 and taking his side safely over the 200-mark. But it had been a most encouraging England show, coming after Edgbaston, and no one had been more impressive than Ian Botham. He had claimed the wickets of Greenidge, Haynes, Gomes, Richards and Lloyd – the entire top half of the West Indies batting – and he later chipped in to dismiss Dujon for 8, Harper for 8 and his Somerset colleague Joel Garner for 6. He had taken eight wickets for 103, the best analysis returned by an England bowler in a home Test against the West Indies and the second time he had taken eight wickets for England at Lord's. With that performance he joined Mankad, Laker, Tayfield, Massie, Imran Khan and Kapil Dev, the only other players to have taken eight wickets twice in a Test match at Lord's.

So the underdogs gained a small advantage over the West Indies on first innings, and there seemed everything to play for.

Lloyd's summing-up of the match at that point was that England had done exceptionally well, and he recalled his original assessment that it can be futile to write off an England Test team playing at home, no matter how vulnerable they may at first appear. He felt his quick bowlers would have to bowl accurately and strike early if England were not to turn a relatively minor advantage into a significant major one.

England's start to their second innings was poor. Broad, who had defended so stubbornly the first time round, was caught off Garner for a 'duck' and when 28 runs later Fowler departed leg-before to Milton Small, who had been brought into the side as fourth seam bowler in place of the injured Holding, the West Indies had as good as wiped out the advantage England had gained on first innings. Gower picked up a few here and there but always looked vulnerable against the fast rising ball outside the offstump. His often intemperate flashes there gave the West Indians all the encouragement they needed. His end was predictable. Playing at a ball from Small which appeared to start on offstump and move away just a shade, he was picked up at slip by a jubilant Clive Lloyd. England were 36 for 3 and in trouble. When Mike Gatting was out for the second time in the match padding up to Malcolm Marshall without offering a stroke, the view rapidly took hold that some kind of collective misfortune, or worse still, madness had besieged the England camp.

Allan Lamb kept his head down and maintained his concentration throughout a sometimes dour innings. He got stuck in the 50s for the better part of an hour but seemed unconcerned by shouts that he should 'get on with it'. And he was probably right, because England's lead was approaching 300, there was still some batting to come, and these were runs the West Indies would have to make to win the Test. While Lamb struggled with extreme caution, the great Botham was being his extravagant best, making 81. With every flourish of his powerful bat he advertised his stomach for the fight. He lifted the fast bowlers over midwicket with astonishing lack of regard, and slowly, by degrees, he forced Lloyd onto the defensive.

A great surprise it was, then, when with just under an hour left for play on the Monday evening Lamb and Pringle opted for the easy life and decided to come off for bad light. England were then 328 runs ahead, by no means an inconsequential target in itself. It later emerged that the players had taken the decision without the benefit of any guidance from the England dressing-room, and there was a footling discussion about where the England captain had been at the time and whether he should not have been paying more attention to the progress of the match from a visible position on the balcony. But the deed had been done; the West Indies left the field grateful to know that they would not be asked to bat in that light, and England resumed the following day. There were two consequences of England's tactics, if such they were. They lost the best bowling conditions when they had to continue batting on the final day; and they revealed that they were still not quite prepared to be seen to push the West Indians into a corner.

In his hotel room that evening Clive Lloyd was in no doubt about the size of the West Indies task to make the runs, but he was also relieved not to have been put in that Monday evening, when Ian Botham might have been at his best. The West Indies were left to make 344 runs to win or to keep their wickets to avoid defeat.

What was to be one of the more famous days in the entire history of West Indies cricket began quietly. In the first thirty minutes only ten

runs came, and just after the West Indies negotiated the first 50 runs
Desmond Haynes was not quick enough to beat Lamb's underarm
throw from square-leg. 57 for 1.

That was the last England success. Gordon Greenidge, playing the
innings of his life, demonstrating masterly technique and invincible
concentration, began to assume command of the England bowling. At
the other end Larry Gomes flicked and pushed ones and twos and
very soon looked untroubled. As the England bowling lost its zest,
Greenidge's assurance became total. He was vicious against anything
short. His flashing square-drives left the fielders immobile. Anything
short on the onside was hoisted over the stands.

In four hours of unforgettable batting Greenidge scored an undefeated 214. He had been given much of the strike by the self-effacing
Gomes (who was not out 92 when the West Indies overhauled their
target to win the second Test), yet had faced only 242 balls. He hit 29
fours and two sixes and became the first West Indian ever to score a
double century at Lord's. Only Bradman and Hammond had done
better on that ground.

There were some dimensions of Greek tragedy in the manner of
England's defeat. They had led on first innings and had done sufficiently well in their second to attempt to go for a win by declaring in
their second innings. Not since 1948 had England lost a Test match
after a second-innings declaration.

Lloyd could find no compliments too great to describe Greenidge's
double century, his first in Test cricket and the one which took him
past 4,000 runs in his 54th Test match.

> It was a tremendous performance. He paced it well, concentrated
> well, went after the loose deliveries and played the innings of his life.
> Gordon is a great player and it was a pleasure to see him come good
> just when we needed it. England didn't play badly; Ian Botham
> bowled well; in the first innings Fowler batted well and Lamb got a
> good hundred in the second, but we stuck to our task; it was a
> workmanlike West Indies performance. We had talked about the
> way we were going to approach the final day at our team meeting
> and it all worked. In fact, it worked a little better than we
> anticipated. It's a great pleasure to go into the third Test two-up. But
> we shan't relax.

Not since 1921, and only twice in the history of their game, had
England ever lost the first three Test matches in a row at home, and the

odds against any side getting the better of an England team to such an extent, when the vagaries of the English summer are taken into account, must be remote.

But England had been stunned by the cruel fate that had befallen them at Lord's; and the sports writers had again written the team's obituary with a conspicuous lack of charity. But as John Bunyan wrote, 'He that is down needs fear no fall', and the England captain must have approached the third encounter with the West Indies at Headingley believing that perhaps the worst had passed.

Gower won the toss and decided to bat, but again the West Indies quick bowlers struck early, powerful blows. Fowler hung around for half an hour and made ten runs, with much unease, before he was beaten for sheer pace and was lbw to Joel Garner. Paul Terry, making his début, did not last as long; he scored eight runs before he fell to Holding. That was 43 for 2. Ten runs later, David Gower was trapped in front by Garner before he got into his stride. By lunch on the first day, England were three down for 68.

But Lamb came in to stop the rot and first with Broad and then with Botham, who scored 45, began to steer England to a semblance of respectability. But the West Indies four pace bowlers gave the England batsmen no let-up. Marshall was amazingly quick; Holding deadly accurate; Garner almost impossible to play; and Baptiste nagged away on a good length with sufficient determination to exploit the slightest error on the part of the batsman. This was what Lloyd's philosophy was all about. Occasionally he would bowl Harper. The tall, elegant Guyanese offspinner had 19 overs in England's first innings and was rewarded with three wickets. But the bulk of the attack went to the fast men. When Broad was caught, picked up at first-slip by the unerring Lloyd, England were 87 for 4. The best partnership of the match between Lamb and Botham took England to within shouting distance of 200, but when Lamb went for an even 100 the rest of the batting quickly folded. England's 270 was clearly not good enough.

And yet in their reply the West Indies were only marginally better. Paul Allott, making his comeback to Test cricket, bowled a perfect length and line on a wicket which proved to his liking, and the persistent Willis bowled his heart out as usual. Only Gomes of the West Indian players proved phlegmatic enough not to be tempted by the accurate line of the England seamers. When Richards, a trifle impatiently, was caught at mid-on by Pringle off Allott, the West Indies were pulled back from being 78 for 3 to 148 for 4 by another model knock from Clive Lloyd. He came to within two runs of his fifty before he was out. Gomes batted throughout for 104 and the West Indies led England by 32 runs on first innings. That they achieved a lead at all was due to an extraordinary display of Sunday league hitting from Michael Holding near the close of the innings. In 55 minutes he hit Willis for five sixes and struck three fours which took the West Indies from 206 for 7 to 288 for 8. It seemed the moment when England finally believed that the gods were not on their side.

They certainly failed to help when England batted a second time. By stumps on the third day they were reeling at 135 for 6, hopelessly outclassed and totally out of the reckoning. Fowler made 50 and Gower, rediscovering something like his old form, stayed long enough to make 43. But that was that. As if to emphasise their psychological advantage, Malcolm Marshall, who had come out to bat one-handed (he had a broken thumb) to ensure that Gomes got his century in the first innings, now bowled with venom to better his record earlier in the series with an analysis of seven wickets for 53 runs off 29 overs. When the West Indian opening stand reached 100 without loss, the deficit faced by the West Indies – 131 – looked simple. The runs were achieved with the loss of just two wickets, and England had been beaten by eight.

Lloyd tried to offer words of consolation to English supporters. He asserted that England were not the only side to have gone through a bad patch. 'The West Indies went 21 Tests without winning,' he said, 'but we kept shuffling the players until we found the right ones. England must look to young players.'

The response from some English cricket commentators was bitter. This England team is not an old one. What England needs now is quality, not age.

At Old Trafford in the fourth Test the West Indies had decidedly the better of a wicket which looked dry from the first morning of the match and which was therefore likely to assist spin bowling. That the West Indies were able to call on offspinner Roger Harper, when the wicket did give some assistance to his off-breaks, was evidence if any were needed of the balanced nature of the team which toured England in 1984.

Harper's bowling aside, the record books will show that the man of the match was again Gordon Greenidge, who made a second double century and just when his team needed it most. When Lloyd was caught behind off the bowling of Paul Allott for a single, the West Indies were in dire straits at 70 for 4. Greenidge added 197 runs with Dujon, who reached his century before he fell to Botham, and then against all expectations added another 170 with Winston Davis, who had been sent in as nightwatchman and who had not even been in the original West Indian squad of players. England's embarrassment was at its most acute as Greenidge progressed with assurance and Davis hit the ball all over the place to notch up ten fours in his score of 77. The ovation he received when he lost his wicket with the West Indies score at 437 would have done credit to Bradman or Sobers.

After batting for ten hours the West Indies were all out for 500, Greenidge having been out for 223.

A near-capacity crowd was at Old Trafford to see England respond to the challenge posed by West Indies' formidable total. And there was a lot for England supporters to cheer about when play began after lunch. Fowler and Broad put on 90 runs for the first-wicket partnership before Winston Davis struck the first blow. Fending off a Davis bouncer, Broad was caught in the slips by Harper. He had made 42. After that, England had only one cause to celebrate – the batting of Lamb. Paul Terry's arm had been broken by Davis. When the innings closed for 280, a long way behind the West Indies, Lamb was undefeated with 100. He had reached 98 when Paul Terry, with his arm in a sling, was sent out, not only to see Lamb to his well-deserved hundred but to try to avoid having to follow on. But then Lamb took the chance of getting his hundred instead of saving Terry from the strike and England were made to follow on after all.

Their second innings was an unmitigated disaster. England were all out after 66 overs for 156, losing the fourth Test by an innings and 64 runs. Harper's six wickets for 57 runs made him the first West Indian spinner in 22 years (since Lance Gibbs) to take six wickets in a Test innings against England. In ideal conditions he had bowled superbly and only Gordon Greenidge's double century robbed Harper of the Man of the Match award.

The only question surrounding the fifth and final Test match at the Oval was whether the West Indies would win all five Test matches in the series, a feat which had never been accomplished by the West Indies – and only twice before in the history of Test cricket (Australia v England in 1920–21 and England v India in 1959). When Lloyd's team succeeded without a great deal of trouble, West Indies plunged into one long night of celebrations.

On his way to take part in several radio and television postmortems on the tour, Clive Lloyd passed a magnum of champagne to his wife, sitting just below the players' balcony, and the corks popped freely in the crowded West Indies dressing-room. It was more than fitting that such an historic honour should have come to the West Indies under the leadership of its longest serving and most distinguished captain. At the beginning of the year he had been fêted in the West Indies for playing his 100th Test match. Nearing its end he had led the West Indies on an historic tour of England.

Lloyd refuses to accept some of the more conventional judgements for England's poor showing. He sees it as a culmination of a number of factors, the chief of which is the quality of English wickets:

People become too preoccupied with things like over-rates and so on. You can bowl 100 or more overs in a day and the game could still be boring. The main point is that wickets should be better. You can't play good cricket on bad wickets. In the early seventies there were some very good wickets and the cricket showed that. Then suddenly someone decided that it might not be a bad idea to have 'sporting wickets', and suddenly survival took over from skill. A batsman's chief concern then was to be able to hang on. That does not produce good cricket. If wickets are well prepared, batsmen could play their shots. If they are underprepared, then they can't. A great deal is talked about the way young English batsmen play the game. I am convinced that young players want to strike the ball. People want to see the ball hit – cricket played in an enjoyable manner: good bowling, good batting, on wickets conducive to decent cricket. English players can strike the ball just as well as West Indian players, but they must be given the wickets on which they can do that. You can't play shots on soft pudding-like English surfaces. There is, of course, the question too of attitudes. People tend to concentrate on a batsman's defence in England. In the West Indies, if a fellow strikes the ball well, we never discourage him. We do try to build his defence, that's true, but batsmen are encouraged to hit the ball. So that a player learns to do both, to build up his defence, but also to keep hitting the ball. Players must never be discouraged from being aggressive. That, I think, is the difference between cricket in England and in the West Indies. People concentrate on too many peripheral reasons.

There is another consequence of unprepared wickets. The grass is occasionally cut so low, right down to the roots, that the bounce becomes unpredictable. The ball, striking at some parts of a wicket like that, either flies or stands up. When players come up against real pace like the West Indies quick bowlers, they can't cope. These wickets have spoilt good cricket. There's been the feeling around that the way you make two teams more equal is by the wicket you prepare. You know, you say, they have quick bowlers, let's prepare a slow wicket. That almost amounts to cheating.

And should anyone believe that Lloyd is talking only from the perspective of a captain with an abundance of quick bowling talent from which to choose, then these words from the former England fast bowler, Bob Willis, might be instructive. In his book *Fast Bowling with Bob Willis*, the one-time England captain has this to say:

Not enough youngsters have the resilience to say to themselves, 'I know I can bowl fast, and I'm going to work at it'. On English wickets, you can usually get away with bowling little seamers to a defensive field; it invariably works at county level because of the deteriorating quality of wickets, so why should a youngster try extra hard to be a fast bowler when he has watched first-class cricketers opting for conformity?

Ideally, a fast bowler needs a hard quick wicket of even bounce, so that he will be rewarded for putting effort into his bowling. Unfortunately, such wickets are a thing of the past in England.

From almost entirely different perspectives, Lloyd and Willis are saying the same thing. While English cricket has been 'opting for conformity', Lloyd has pushed his West Indian players to a professionalism and an excellence which has demolished those who seek only to conform. And, in the end, that perhaps was the message of England's demise in 1984.

Lloyd himself is in no doubt about it. His view:

Surely, we had for about ten years or so a squad of immensely talented players. But they were individuals and had to be moulded into a team. And with that our cricket became more mature; my first task was to kill the notion that we were simply a bunch of happy-go-lucky calypso cricketers. A more analytical approach to our cricket was needed. We placed great emphasis on physical fitness. We worked generally for the betterment of our cricket in the sense that we took a little bit of time to think about our game and analyse what was needed to improve. We talked about these things. We were not going to be content to go out there simply trying to be flamboyant players. We are more professional in outlook. And I think this in part stems from being county cricketers in England as well. One other point is important. Young players must be given a chance to establish themselves. When I started I don't think young players got as many chances ... When I took over the captaincy, I used my position to make players relax so that they can go out and play without the nervous thought in their minds that if they failed once, they'd never play again. A lot of our players have had a longer time to establish themselves than any other players have had before. The pattern of my captaincy of the West Indies team was to a great extent dictated by the fact that the game is so terribly important for us in the Caribbean. It's much more than a game. It carries with it all sorts of aspirations and hopes of West Indian people. The key to the West Indies captaincy is realising all that.

It could not have been put better by M. A. Noble himself, one of the famous Australian captains. He said: 'The great leader is the embodiment of all the hopes, virtues, courage and ability possessed by the ten men under his command. If he is not he is but a shadow and lacks the substance of captaincy. He will not last.'

Lloyd showed all the necessary qualities and as a result lasted longer than any other player or captain in the history of the game. However, he has a genuine soft spot for the England captain David Gower and feels that the Leicestershire left-hander should have been given the captaincy of the England team in 1982 after Keith Fletcher.

In June of that year Lloyd wrote in a British newspaper:

I just can't understand the reasoning of the English selectors over the Test captaincy. They have chosen to get rid of Keith Fletcher, one of the shrewdest and most experienced skippers in the game.

They have replaced him with Bob Willis, who has had a lot of injury problems and who is certainly not a longterm prospect. And worst of all they have ignored the obvious claims of David Gower, who should have been given six home Tests [against the Indians] in which to pave the way for next winter's tour of Australia.

In his article the West Indies captain outlined what he felt were the reasons for giving Gower the responsibility of leading the England side. He wrote:

Gower has had a long apprenticeship under Brearley, Botham and Fletcher. But surely the selectors ought to be looking for a longterm captain, particularly after all the chopping and changing of the last few years.

It's obvious that at some stage Gower has been groomed for the England job . . . why haven't they given it to him this season against India . . . Instead, they have made the mistake of picking a stopgap captain and robbed Gower of any chance of learning his job in easy conditions. That way there would not be the pressure on him as there was when Botham began against Australia and the West Indies.

At the end of the 1984 series between England and the West Indies, Lloyd stuck to his view. Charitably, he felt that even in the fire of international cricket competition it was perhaps unfortunate that in his first series as captain Gower should have run up against a West Indies side in such irrepressible form.

Lloyd was magnanimous in victory but annoyed at the resurrection of the view that the decline of English cricket had been caused by the number of overseas players in the county game in England. He says:

That idea, which is always being brought up these days, is total nonsense. You have two or three hundred county players and twenty or thirty overseas players. It is silly to argue that those overseas players keep out prospective England ones. England should be able from the number of county players to find at least fourteen top-class players. It's not a realistic argument to blame it all on overseas players.

CHAPTER ELEVEN
Captain of Champions

West Indies have had two great captains ... Frank
Worrell and Clive Lloyd. Like Worrell, Lloyd is a
father figure to his team and ... that is exactly what
they need.

Richie Benaud

Richie Benaud's words – 'exactly what they need' – make an important beginning for any discussion about how good a captain Clive Lloyd has been. Before any controversy, though, some facts are self-evident. Under the leadership of Clive Lloyd, the West Indies cricket team has never known such success. Moreover, few captains in the history of the game have been more successful. When Lloyd led his triumphant team to an historic five-nil victory against England at the Oval in August 1984, he had led the West Indies 69 times, and in his last 36 Tests only one had been lost. And that, as Jim Swanton wrote, was 'on what Plum Warner used to call a "false" pitch at Melbourne at Christmas 1981'.

The West Indies under Lloyd have been the strongest side in the world for nearly ten years. In that time England have won only one match against them out of the last 28 and have been beaten 13 times. Australia have been beaten nine times out of 16 and have won only twice. Lloyd has not only led the West Indies as captain, he has contributed to his team's overall performance with his individual contribution: over 7,100 runs in 166 Test innings, 18 centuries, 37 scores of 50 or more and 85 catches. In his own right he has come to be regarded as a towering figure in the world of cricket. One incidental statistic reminds us that in his day there was no more fearsome hitter of the cricket ball; he shares with G. L. Jessop the record for the fastest 200 in the history of the game.

Comparisons with other West Indies captains are barely worth making. Sobers led the West Indies in 39 Tests, winning nine of them and losing ten. Twenty were drawn. John Goddard, who brought the victorious West Indies team to England in 1950, won eight Tests, lost seven and drew seven. Gerry Alexander, who became captain of the West Indies team when many felt Frank Worrell should have been given the job long before, won seven of the 18 Tests in which he led the team, lost four and drew seven. And Frank Worrell's record was: 15 Tests, nine won, three lost, two drawn and one ending in the famous tie against Australia at Brisbane.

Lloyd was the first West Indies captain ever to win a series in Australia. Former captains Grant in 1930–31, Goddard in 1951–52, Worrell in 1960–61, Sobers in 1968–69 and Lloyd himself in 1975–76 were all beaten 'down under'. Strange as it may seem, no other West Indian captain had ever won a series in Pakistan before Lloyd did just that in 1980. And incredible though it may appear, when Lloyd beat England in the West Indies in 1981 by two Tests to nil, he became the first West Indian captain to accomplish that feat since 1948.

Yet doubts about the quality of Lloyd's leadership remain, some from opponents who have suffered terribly at the hands of the West Indies, some from informed observers of the game, some even from his own players.

First, though, Benaud's point. Lloyd was exactly the kind of captain the West Indies needed – a father figure. Benaud adds: 'When they are captained otherwise, they tend to move back to the excitable individual state of years gone by and there is less responsibility in their cricket.'

The tendency to be 'excitable' and to show occasionally 'less responsibility' than they should is a frequent criticism of the West Indian approach to cricket. The players themselves dislike it and can hardly be prevailed upon to assess its merit calmly, but there can be no doubt that under Lloyd the West Indies team has assumed a more professional outlook.

The purists may continue to beat their chests in agony, but it was to Packer's World Series Cricket that the West Indies owe most in this regard. The reason for this was simple enough. For years, West Indian Test players complained to their Board about their meagre rewards for playing the most exciting Test cricket on the world circuit. The Board, perennially strapped for funds, had never been able fully to reward their players for the job. In stepped Kerry Packer, who offered West Indians a small fortune for taking part in his renegade series. There was only one qualification. They had to be 'professional'. Packer was obsessed by that word and he conveyed his obsession to his players. For the first time in their lives, West Indian players were made to attend lectures and mini-seminars by Australian sports professionals, like tennis star John Newcombe, on how to get the best out of their game. Winning teams earned more money under Packer, and since their low rates of pay had always been the West Indians' prime complaint they embraced the new system with alacrity.

It was not all voluntary, either. One of the West Indies players tells the story of Packer's version of 'play or else'. He would say to recalcitrant players: 'You have a chance to play well, give a thousand per cent and make more money than you ever have before. If you decide that is not what you want to do, a Quantas flight leaves Sydney every day.' The West Indies players took the point and carried it over into the rest of their cricket. In the 1984 series against England, there was not a man on the tour who would not strain every nerve to smash England into the ground. Commentators frequently remark how different West Indian players are when they are playing for the West Indies. The difference is that Clive Lloyd and all the other senior ex-Packer players drive the team to higher and higher achievements. Playing for Packer, that meant money. Today, the rewards for being part of a victorious team might not be as great but they are still more substantial than they have ever been. The players know that. It is the lesson Clive Lloyd has driven into them. The response of people like Malcolm Marshall speaks for itself.

During Test matches vice-captain Viv Richards sits on a chair in the pavilion or on some prominent balcony urging his team-mates on, 'Come on, make it two . . . make it two', 'Go on, Maco [to Marshall], there's more than one run in that', and when a player fails to take advantage of tardy fielding Richards' impatience borders on down-right intolerance.

That is part of the legacy of Kerry Packer. Hear Gordon Greenidge on the subject. Writing in 1980, he said:

The West Indians [in the Packer World Series Cricket] got off to a slow start and lost some early matches. Kerry Packer called a meeting of West Indian players and told us to improve in no uncertain terms. I improved tremendously . . . I ceased to become one of the West Indies happy hookers and I learnt to concentrate more.

Richards adds:

Sure, we were told we have to give of our best. That was that. If we didn't, we knew what the consequences would be. It gave us all the incentive to play better, to strive for every run, for every wicket, for every victory. There was, of course, professional pride in winning too. After all, we were up against some of the best cricketers in the world and when you are, you do try and play your best. But the point was as well, we were being well paid to play well. Cricketers were no longer the poor relations of sportsmen. So, sure, we had to do our best.

Throughout this period of West Indies cricket, Lloyd, the 'father figure' as Benaud calls him, played the dominant role. His was the voice the players respected. He decided the Packer venture was worth trying, said so and the West Indies players followed him to Australia. He walked out when the West Indies Board failed to justify their exclusion of certain Packer players during an Australian tour of the Caribbean, and senior players like Richards and Garner needed only a telephone call before they did the same, following their captain and precipitating a crisis which nearly denuded West Indies cricket of its richest talent.

Benaud is also alluding to the fact that, because of their composition, West Indies cricket teams are notoriously difficult to lead. And, as Frank Worrell observed, a captain's talent in the West Indies lay in blending the different personalities from the different islands into one cohesive unit. That requires not a technical mastery of the game but a kind of unruffleable temperament, a quiet but strongly influential force. Clive Lloyd has that and so earned the respect of his players. On his last tour of India it was almost moving to see two or three players competing to carry out an order from their captain. One of them was observed late one afternoon cutting Lloyd's hair. Lloyd's teams would do almost anything for him. It may not be necessary for other teams to have that kind of relationship with their captain. In the case of West Indies teams, though, it is certainly a great help.

Yet questions have been asked about his ability under pressure – even by his own players. In his book *The Man in the Middle*, published in 1980, Gordon Greenidge made known his views. To the best of this writer's knowledge, Greenidge has not changed his mind. Greenidge wrote:

It is my opinion alone, but I do not think Clive Lloyd will go down in history as one of the great inspirational leaders. Clive, a marvellous and instinctive cricketer, was the captain of a great team or potentially a great team. I mean no criticism when I say that a more natural leader could have turned us into the most outstanding of all post-war teams.

When we were losing heavily and so disappointingly in Australia
in 1975–76, Lloyd found it impossible to lift us individually or
collectively and was as bemused and shattered as the rest of us when
Australia went on to win 5–1, with as much ease as the scoreline
suggests. There have been times when the West Indies have been
doing well, when an old-age pensioner could captain us. All the
skipper needs to do when we are getting runs is to maintain
momentum. This Clive did, but I can think of few real instances
when his shrewd leadership changed the course of a match. I do not
think Lloyd ranks with Brearley or Greig as captain. He has not
always been able to motivate a losing side.

Adding a more personal note to his observations, Greenidge wrote:
'He has done nothing to help me, reserving his comments about me for
newspapers.'

For his part, Lloyd sticks by his version of the 1975–76 tour of
Australia. The West Indies were taken apart by a very fine pace attack.
There had been some careless West Indies cricket, and there had been a
number of questionable umpiring incidents. But by and large, Lloyd
admits, the West Indies were the architects of their own disaster.

None of this, though, answers Greenidge's point about whether
Lloyd is capable of pulling his team together in the face of a string of
continuing bad performances. The plain fact is that under his leadership there have been few such patches.

But the point will not go away. One way to attempt to dispose of it is
to assert that it cannot always be argued that brilliant teams run
themselves. Nor is it true that brilliant captains are immune from bad
patches. Peter May's 1958–59 team to Australia suffered almost as
badly as the West Indies did seventeen years later.

May's side lost the Ashes by four matches to nil. Yet months before
the tour *Wisden* solemnly expressed the view that 'Peter May's
achievements are without parallel'. *Wisden*'s prelude to the Australian
tour continued:

Never before has the same man led England through a series of Test
matches and his country to the top of the Championship in the same
year. Clearly England stand at the top of the cricket world. Rarely
has our prestige been so high. There are some who aver that England
has never possessed a better side, but in making comparisons one
must remember conditions have changed. Pitches are certainly very
different in this country and in Australia compared with 20 years

ago. Tactics too have changed with a leaning on occasions towards defensive bowling. The reason for England's present success is possession of a fine captain, a fine array of bowlers suited to all types of pitches and the way these men have been brilliantly supported on the field. Also adequate reserves have been available when first choices have withdrawn.

Although it might be felt with hindsight that *Wisden* succumbed to hyperbole, May's 1958–59 team did look impressive on paper: Richardson, Graveney, Dexter, Cowdrey, Bailey, Evans, Lock, Laker, Trueman, Statham, Loader et al. But the team was given a fearful thrashing by the Australians.

So Lloyd would maintain that he is not the only competent captain to be put to the sword by a better side. And he does make the point that the logical extension of Greenidge's argument would be to say that no good or successful captain ever loses a Test match. That contention is not borne out by the records.

Besides, Greenidge's strictures apart, other West Indian players tell a different story. The promising Guyanese offspinner, Roger Harper, would credit a great deal of his success on the 1984 England tour to the encouragement and inspiration of his captain. Harper, over six feet tall, was encouraged by his captain not to hurl the ball down from his great height but to spin and loop his deliveries, making the most advantage of his height.

And the heir-in-waiting, Viv Richards, disquieted though he may have been at times as to whether Lloyd would ever give up the captaincy so that he, Richards, might achieve his ambition to lead the West Indies, freely admits that 'Clive has been an inspiration to us all'.

But the most trenchant charges against Clive Lloyd have concerned his over-dependence on quick bowling. Brian Close, former Yorkshire and England captain, says flatly that Lloyd can hardly be considered a great captain because he has not shown himself able to handle a spin attack. This is another way of saying that it is all too easy to 'rotate' four pace bowlers.

Bob Willis says in his book *The Cricket Revolution*: 'In my opinion he [Lloyd] has never been a great captain by any stretch of the imagination . . . Clive Lloyd's tactics . . . have in my view produced a boring formula that has made his team world champions.'

After suffering at the hands of the West Indian pace bowlers in the West Indies, Sunil Gavaskar, the Indian captain, shares Willis' views. He says: 'Lloyd was desperate and he touched a new low in a desperate effort to win by having all our eleven players hospitalised by his pace bowlers. This was not great captaincy, it was barbarism.'

The point about Lloyd's over-dependence on quick bowling, it seems, will not go away. Two things must be said about it, not necessarily in Lloyd's defence, but they must be stated as simple facts.

The first is that the entire West Indies team under Clive Lloyd has been converted to the theory of the effectiveness of having three or four quick bowlers in the side. That emerges most clearly at team meetings before Test matches, where vice-captain Viv Richards would usually say when the question of variety in the attack comes up for discussion: 'I don't think we need any spinners. Should there be the call for spin variation during the match, Larry [Gomes] and I can bowl a few overs.'

While neither Richards nor Gomes would regard themselves as top-class spin bowlers, it is easy to see, from Richards' point of view, why the West Indies reject out of hand any criticisms of the West Indies attack being unbalanced or too dependent on fast bowling. The quickies, it is true, will perform for the major part of the game. But should circumstances demand a change, the Richards' argument would be that the team is equipped to cope. And, of course, Lloyd would ridicule the theory that slow bowlers must occasionally be brought in purely in the name of variety.

The second point is that when Guyana won the Shell Shield trophy in the West Indies in 1983, Lloyd led a team with no fewer than four spin bowlers, including Roger Harper. So that, contrary to what is generally believed, he is capable of switching his spin bowlers around just as much as he does with his quicker men.

It is left to the current England captain, David Gower, to put some perspective on criticisms about Lloyd's leadership. Gower says:

> As a captain, Clive cannot have been too disappointed to have at his disposal the most fearsome attack let loose on Test cricket. Never before have four genuinely quick bowlers lined up on the same side. Most of the time, all Clive has had to do is to wind them up and let them go, with the occasional few overs of spin from Richards or Gomes to provide relief when necessary, or to precipitate the arrival of the second new ball. It's not often they have needed the third new ball in recent years!

And to those who would dispense with Lloyd's captaincy on the basis that it lacks tactical skill, Gower goes on:

Whatever one might say about Clive's tactical skills, and there are those who claim them to be limited, he has been the West Indies' most enduring and successful captain, so to carp about his leadership seems almost churlish.

The captaincy requires a certain amount of diplomatic skill within the team, for inter-island rivalries still play a part in West Indies cricket politics. There are always personalities in that part of the world who would need to be subdued, at some stage or other, for the good of the team.

Clive seems to have managed that so successfully that he has won tremendous respect not only from his own people and players, but from people around the world. Clive Lloyd has been a delight to play against.

The arguments about Lloyd's tactical skill will perhaps continue as long as the game is played. There can be no argument, however, as Gower says, about Lloyd's performance in the job. He has never believed in defensive tactics, although he has at times employed them. Aggression is his natural game, although perhaps on occasions his quick bowlers have come close to infringing the law about intimidatory bowling. He has always been without doubt the man in charge of his team.

When England went to Australia in 1982–83, the England captain, Bob Willis, described how one decision to put the opposition in to bat had been arrived at. He wrote later:

It would be an understatement to say I was surprised when I discovered that I was in the minority. Every player consulted came up with the same view – we should bowl. In my heart, I knew we should be doing it for all the wrong reasons, negative reasons, because the batsmen plainly did not fancy batting against the pace bowlers . . . I had to adopt a tongue-in-cheek attitude to explain my decision.

Lloyd says about that incident:

A captain must lead and cannot expect to make decisions by committee. Certainly, there are times when senior players are consulted. But whether you bat or not and things like that, that's the captain's responsibility and no one else's.

Leading the West Indies in the field, though, has been but one aspect of Lloyd's work as captain. E. W. Swanton has written that Lloyd 'naturally and unself-consciously fulfils an ambassadorial role between the West Indies and his adopted country'. At the end of the 1984 tour of England, Lloyd was off to the West Indies in anticipation of the problems which might be caused in the West Indies by the almost inevitable return to the England Test team of Gooch, Emburey and others. England's next tour of the Caribbean is in 1986, and between now and then attempts are being made to resolve the issue of whether Gooch and the others will be acceptable to certain Caribbean governments. It was not surprising that 'ambassador' Lloyd should be involved in the discussions in the Caribbean. He is regarded by governments in the region as no England cricketer can hope to be seen in Westminster.

Lloyd also has a vision of what West Indies cricket should be in the future, and what must be done to make that vision a reality. In 1982 he submitted a paper to West Indian governments warning about the possible recruitment of West Indian players by South African commercial interests. It proved prophetic, but his thoughtful treatment of the issue makes it worthwhile to quote Lloyd's 'position paper' at length. Lloyd wrote:

> Recent rumours, reports and common sense all indicate that serious efforts are now being made, or will shortly be made, by South African interests to have other well-known West Indies players follow the lead of Alvin Kallicharran in playing and coaching in that country. It is clear also that these interests . . . have large resources at their disposal and are backed directly or indirectly by the resources of the South African government itself. It is equally clear that several West Indian players, many of whom do not live in the Caribbean and are thus not directly aware of the political and social climate, and many who do not have a secure future when their playing days are over . . . may be tempted to respond favourably to these offers. General discussions with cricketers, most of whom are English and unsophisticated in the world of public affairs, also revealed feelings that they think that cricket in particular is being made a scapegoat, while the problem is largely a political and economic one and is not being tackled at those levels.
>
> Insofar as the South African government is behind the offer that is being made, the cricketers do appear to have a point, although they are largely unaware of the political and economic steps that have to be taken or the complexities involved in dealing with a

government with vast resources and a totally ruthless attitude to match.

If members of what might be considered the West Indies first and second elevens were to give in to the considerable temptations that could be offered, the implications for both West Indies and world cricket could be grave. The West Indies cricket team is still, at the present time, the world's best and it has been for most of the past six years. The successful recruitment programme by the South Africans would immediately change the situation, probably permanently, since any group that were to respond to the offer would probably be followed by others to whom the temptations would seem just as attractive and less risky.

Lloyd's analysis went on to make a point about the positive value of West Indian cricket to the islands in the Caribbean as a major unifying force, even at times when political considerations have tended to split the territories apart. And he also argued forcefully about the other consequences of widespread West Indian participation in South African 'rebel' tours.

If West Indians do go to South Africa, Australians would almost certainly follow . . . and international cricket as we know it might well come to an end unless the South Africans are re-admitted on what would virtually be their own terms.

The problem is a political and economic one and requires a political and economic solution . . . It would be idle to pretend that the Caribbean could hope to match the scale of the South African offers . . . but if an attractive offer of alternative employment is provided, cricketers would then be put on the spot if they were to take up offers to go to South Africa.

Having identified the problem and its consequences, Lloyd suggested a solution. He got the chance finally to put it to the governments of the region and to the West Indies Board because of the South African recruitment programme. In fact, it is a plan which he began advocating long before Kerry Packer set the organising bodies of international cricket in turmoil with his World Series Cricket.

It is suggested [Lloyd wrote] that a scheme along the following lines could be adopted. There are about 20 to 25 players or two full teams from all the territories who are attractive enough for the South

Africans to make them substantial offers. If each of these could be offered a stipend in the range of US $20,000 – $30,000 in the currency of their own territory in the off season, they could then be assigned to the local board who would use their services both in domestic competitions, for coaching and other purposes. This sum of money could be provided for some three to five years until the International Cricket Conference could tackle the larger problems and specific issues presented by the new South African strategy.

The Lloyd plan was never fully implemented by the West Indies Board, or more precisely by the West Indian governments at which it was aimed. But new and successful methods of sponsoring West Indies cricket were canvassed and more money is being found. Far more to the point, though, is that the plan identified Clive Lloyd's concern with the future of the game in the region, and it is difficult to believe that he will be lost to the administration of cricket in the Caribbean when his own playing days come to an end. One possibility is that he might become a permanent manager of the West Indies team, its ambassador abroad, the eyes and ears of the interest of the West Indies game. It is an idea many West Indian players would welcome.

On the broader issue of sporting contacts with South Africa, Clive Lloyd is in the mainstream of contemporary Caribbean thought. He has addressed a committee of the United Nations in New York on the subject, and his speech there gives the broadest possible hint that perhaps some political involvement in the West Indies lies somewhere in Lloyd's future.

Speaking at the UN he said:

I adhere to the principle of non-discrimination in sport. I cannot and will not compromise on it for any financial gain or for any other consideration. Racism is contrary to the United Nations Charter; it is contrary to humanity . . . It is my personal conviction that to the extent that I play before separate audiences and separate spectators, to that extent I make a direct contribution to the strengthening of the system of apartheid. My own personal conviction compels me instead to fight for the elimination of that system . . . and that's why it gives me so much pleasure and why I consider it my duty to add my voice from the perspective of the captaincy of the West Indies cricket team to the chorus of condemnation of the system of apartheid. There is, Mr Chairman, only one race in the world, and that is the human race. And it is from this perspective that I will continue to make a contribution on the cricket field to strengthening human solidarity.

His speech called for a strengthening of the Gleneagles Accord, to ensure that there be a more 'categorical statement regarding sporting contacts with South Africa'. And it ended:

Whenever men don their sporting apparel to contest on the field of sport where men choose freely to replace the violence of man with the healthy organisation of athletic competition, and where the only true victors are the human spirit and human brotherhood, that's where I'll stand, firmly committed.

Nothing says more about the inescapable link between the politics of the West Indian islands and their cricket team. Extraordinary as it may sound, no contemporary West Indian captain could fail to speak in identical tones. It is the new spirit of the times in the region, and West Indies cricket and the game's personalities must reflect that.

But in this particular area Clive Lloyd has shouldered his responsibility as captain as no other has done. To Learie Constantine, the honour never came. Frank Worrell's stay at the helm was, alas, all too short. Lloyd has made his tenure count. It has counted on and off the cricket field. His view of the game in the West Indies has never been narrow, never petty or selfish. It has been as large and as benevolent as his mighty frame. He has been a decoration to the game. There have been times when his leadership has seemed too laissez-faire, his grip on team discipline not tight enough. A stern defender of his team, Lloyd would probably not disagree. But his virtues as a leader of men far outstrip his shortcomings. In many instances his vociferous protests about incidents on the cricket field have derived more from his sense of outrage that the game cannot be played fairly than from ill-tempered truculence. He learnt to be competitive and tough, but has never been unsporting. Clive Lloyd has made few enemies, if any, in his twenty years in the game. West Indies cricket is in his debt and the game in general stands uplifted in his name.

It is impossible to think that, when his playing days come to an end, he will be lost to cricket. Should the West Indies fail to make use of their best ambassador ever, some other country, like Australia, almost certainly will.

About the end of his playing days, the latter part of which were spent shouldering the responsibilities of leading Australia, the great Don Bradman wrote in *Farewell to Cricket*:

> I did not profess to be an ideal captain . . . but it would have been sheer cowardice not to stay for as long as I did. There had been times when I found it difficult to keep going and although still not old in the cricket sense, I did not feel capable of standing the strain of another occasion. Whatever inspired me to go, I felt it had been ordained for a greater purpose than the pleasure of success of individuals. It had been my destiny to do what I could for cricket and in my heart I knew I could not have done much more.

The modest Lloyd would hardly wish to equate his record with that of Sir Donald. Moreover, Lloyd is 'old in the cricket sense'. As they were to his own, though, Bradman's words are nonetheless a fitting epitaph to Lloyd's magnificent career.

Whatever decision Clive makes about his future, the views of Waveney, his wife of thirteen years, will play a significant role. They met in England in 1968 and, although Waveney had never heard of the young, bespectacled Guyanese player who had been struggling to find a place in the West Indies team, she was not entirely unfamiliar with the game. Waveney was born in Berbice, where it was impossible not to have heard of those other Guyanese from that part of the country who had made their name playing cricket for Guyana and for the West Indies. The list included Rohan Kanhai, Ivan Madray, Joe Solomon, Alvin Kallicharran and Basil Butcher, who is Waveney's first cousin.

Despite these impeccable credentials Waveney had never been a keen fan. She had seen Sobers once in Berbice and had also seen Lance Gibbs in action, bowling his offspinners in the same game. But that was the beginning and end of her contact with the game before meeting Clive. And although, when she worked in the Customs and Excise Department in Georgetown after being a teacher for some years, Clive dropped in for frequent meetings with her boss, they never met.

Their meeting took place thousands of miles from Guyana in Shepherd's Bush in London. In 1967, the year before they met, Waveney's sister, Zena, who had been living in England, went back to Guyana on holiday and promised her sister a 'trip to England'.

It was to be a holiday [Waveney says] but I liked England and since the only way I could stay was to do something useful, I decided to become a nurse. I applied first to the Bexley Heath Psychiatric Hospital in Kent, and then I got a scholarship. It was one of four granted that year for the particular field I was in and we were trained in psychiatric nursing and general nursing. It was tough, but I did well and the result was that after four years one got the two qualifications, for both branches of nursing.

One evening, one of her friends, Thelma Noble, a nurse, finally convinced her that she should go to a party Mrs Noble was giving at her home in Shepherd's Bush. The invitation and her acceptance was to change her life.

By chance, the flat opposite was owned by Oscar Gibbs, Lance's brother, and Clive Lloyd, Lance's cousin, happened to be at Oscar's that same evening. Mrs Noble's husband Ben had gone across the street to have a drink with the Gibbses. He met their guest and on hearing he was Guyanese suggested that he might like to meet 'a nice Guyanese girl who was visiting' next door. Clive was over in ten minutes and, according to Waveney, who was playing records at the time, 'It was love at first sight.'

That evening, they went to a party in London, danced and talked a great deal. When they left each other Clive insisted that he would remember her telephone number, but didn't and was forced to call the Nobles the next day to remind himself how he could get hold of Waveney. He finally did, and from that moment they talked endlessly, every evening. 'It was terrible really,' says Waveney, 'but I would wait up till two in the morning sometimes if I expected him to call. And we talked for hours. I think we should be awarded Telecom shares for all the time we spent on the telephone.'

On a train journey to Manchester Clive Lloyd proposed. Waveney pleaded for time, but gave in very soon afterwards and they were married in 1971.

She recalls today how their relationship almost never got started. During their first meeting she asked what he did.

'I play cricket,' came the reply.

'Yes,' said Waveney, 'I know that, but what do you do for a living?'

Thirteen years later, she is the perennial cricket widow, and one who has never had her husband home for any two consecutive months at a time. 'It's always been like that, we had no honeymoon, but because of the improved pay and conditions for players since Kerry Packer, wives and children can at least see more of their husbands

when they are on overseas tours in Australia, India or the Caribbean.'
  In their years together Mrs Lloyd's interest in cricket and in her
husband's career have grown steadily.

Clive is very serious about his cricket [she avers]. He thinks about
the game, about problems, a great deal, although he never brings
them home in the sense of talking about them too much. In fact quite
the opposite. He simply goes quiet if something is worrying him.
He's also terribly modest. He never tells me how many runs he's
scored, unless he's asked a specific question. If he calls and I say,
'How did you do today' he'll say 'OK'. And I'll say 'Did you get
runs?' and he'll reply 'Yes'. Not until I ask him a specific question
will he tell me how many runs he scored. On one occasion, I think it
was a Roses match, he scored 100-odd and was Man of the Match,
and I never knew a thing until I saw it in the paper the following day.

For his part Clive respects Waveney's views. When he was
approached by Packer's emissaries in Trinidad in the West Indies
during a Pakistan tour of the Caribbean, the most fortunate thing for
him was that Waveney was there at the time. They were able to talk
about the new idea at length.
  The most frightening moment of both their lives was Clive's injury
in Australia in 1971. Clive had been approached to take part in a series
'down under' which had been quickly organised as a replacement for a
South African tour. Going for a catch off the bowling of Ashley
Mallett, he flung himself at the ball, goal-keeper fashion, and landed in
agony on his shoulder. It took his fellow-fielders some time to realise
that he wasn't about to get up again, because he had acquired a
reputation as a brilliant fieldsman who dived at anything which could
be converted into a 'take' or a wicket. A small crack at the base of the
spine was diagnosed, an injury which responded to a long rest but one
which could have ended his cricket had it been more serious.
  Waveney Lloyd says:

We had been married for less than three months when the Secretary
at Old Trafford, Jack Wood, phoned me with the news of Clive's
injury. I had stayed behind in Manchester, to complete my SRN
exams. It made both of us realise just how easy it is to be put out of
the game by injury.
  But good things come out of bad. To get back into the game after
that lay-off, Clive showed the greatest determination. He was really

dedicated to getting himself fit and showed great stamina. But it did shake us all up a little. It could so easily have been the end of everything.

In contrast the best news of his cricketing career came when he was given the captaincy of the West Indies side. 'He called me up and said he was being asked to be captain,' says his wife. 'Even then there was not a great deal of emotion in his voice, but he was clearly delighted and I think when he came home we opened a bottle of champagne.'

But the occasions when Clive shows any great emotion are rare. His wife says:

He will come home and read, watch TV, or we might go to the cinema. His main interests outside cricket are squash and tennis. We both like going to live shows given by big entertainers and Clive likes jazz. He is politically aware, but hates party politics; he has only voted once in his life and I think that was because I dragged him out. It might be difficult for him to be cut off from cricket altogether when he gives up playing. He currently has a sports consultancy firm with Jack Simmons, which tries to place overseas players in English counties, and that's the kind of involvement with the game I believe he will always have. He is very serious about cricket, about his role in it. He has always been determined that the West Indies game should be better when he leaves it.

CHAPTER TWELVE
Bitter-Sweet Finale

The West Indies are simply twice as good as any other
international team.
    I do not like their tactics. Ultimately the transforma-
tion of a beautiful strategic exercise into a brutal game
. . . will be no good for cricket.

Ian Woolridge,
Daily Mail

Disturbingly discordant sounds followed Clive Lloyd's West Indian
team as they completed their triumphal demolition of David Gower's
England side and the record books and as they set off to meet the
Australians. The fears expressed by the scrupulously fair Ian
Woolridge were taken up by Tony Lewis, who captained England
eight times and who is now a respected journalist and cricket commen-
tator. In an article for the third edition of the *Benson and Hedges
Cricket Year*, Lewis wrote:

> There were warnings of West Indians during the summer in Eng-
> land, but the truth is probably that the strictest application of the
> law would be a sensational volte-face and that the umpires rightly
> fear that their stand would not be supported by the Boards of
> Control.
>   The West Indies barrage of bowling aimed at the man, not the
> stumps, has become habit. The West Indies themselves would be the
> last to appreciate how they have eroded the pleasurable side of
> cricket.

Clive Lloyd's reply to this accusation was not dissimilar to the
response to a German commander's request during the Battle of the
Bulge that the Americans surrender since they were surrounded and in
a hopeless position: 'Nuts!'
    But echoes of the controversy about the deadly effectiveness of the
West Indies fast bowling found their way thousands of miles across the
world when the West Indies reached Australia. Even before Lloyd's
tourists landed, the former Australian Test wicket-keeper Rodney
Marsh told an audience at the National Press Club in Australia that

the West Indies could be beaten if the Australians adopted and stuck to the right strategy.

With typical truculence he explained that strategy:

I would say Plan A is to fight fire with fire . . . in other words, try to crack a few skulls. You know damn well they are going to bowl you bouncers and you know damn well they will run into our tailend batsmen and put a couple around the ribs. Our bowlers have to be able to take that.

Marsh's comments raised a storm of controversy before a single ball was bowled in the series.

Not every commentator shared his view. Richie Benaud sagely observed:

The West Indies have been given a head start in the series by the call that a few skulls should be cracked as a tactic for the summer. Brains are to be put on the back burner.

The West Indies have a great cricket team. That team can be regarded as the goodies if the bumpers start to fly. They are merely responding to the Australians' ridiculous challenge.

They can be beaten and the way to beat them is not through airy-fairy statements but through sheer hard slog and dedication by cricketers who want desperately to walk through brick walls to win, not just to take part.

Rodney Marsh's friend and one-time Australian captain, Ian Chappell, did not agree with Marsh's recipe for success either. He reasoned that a battle of bouncers would not be won or lost by batsmen of either side, adding that such a contest would usually be terminated by the team whose fast bowlers cannot 'stomach the retaliation when it comes their turn to bat'. Chappell continued:

In what would amount to a straight-out battle of will power and grit between Geoff Lawson, Rodney Hogg and Carl Rackemann and Malcolm Marshall, Joel Garner, Michael Holding and Eldine Baptiste, my money would be on the quartet from the Caribbean.

Apart from not being able to win that fight (which I doubt the umpires would allow anyway) Marsh's theory does not make allowance for what effect this would have on the approach of batsmen like Viv Richards, Gordon Greenidge and Clive Lloyd.

Antagonising them by bowling a barrage of bouncers at the West Indies pace bowlers is going to result in their increased desire to exact retribution. I would have thought they present a big enough problem in a happy mood without making them angry and more determined.

The former Australian captain concluded: 'No, Rod, it's beers that are for cracking – heads are for using thoughtfully.'

Clive Lloyd refused to be baited by all this. He had experienced before the tactic of commentators trying to get the better of West Indies teams even before a ball had been bowled. He stated again that people's criticisms of the way the West Indies played the game were ill-informed. And he chided Rodney Marsh for making inflammatory comments from the relative safety of his retirement.

It's amazing [said Lloyd] how when some players finish playing the game, they have such a great deal to say. He [Marsh] never made such statements when he was around in Test cricket. Now that he is no longer there there is all this talk of brutality coming into cricket. That has never been the way the West Indies played the game under me and it never will be. We want to play good, fair cricket and that's just what we'll do here in Australia. We have never set out to injure people. There's really no great point in that. It's all rather silly. We're here to play cricket in the proper spirit.

In the first Test match at Perth that 'proper' West Indian spirit overwhelmed the Australians. The West Indies began their tour by beating the home team by an innings and 112 runs. Lloyd himself was one of two West Indian batsmen who failed to score when his team batted first. But it didn't seem to matter. Centuries from Gomes, his eighth in Tests and one of the slowest ever by a West Indian batsman, and Jeff Dujon gave the West Indies a sound first-innings score of 416.

Australia's reply was pathetic. Holding, reverting to his long run-up, ably supported by Marshall and Garner made mincemeat of the Australian batting. The home side were dismissed for 76 runs in just over 31 overs, their lowest score in 58 Tests between the two countries and their worst performance since 1968. Holding's bowling figures read more like a fairytale than a Test match performance: 9 overs, 3 maidens, 21 runs, 6 wickets.

Australia summoned up more courage when they followed on, but they were still left a long way behind. In 70.3 overs they made 228.

It was the West Indies' fourth consecutive win over Australia in a year and their ninth successive Test victory, which took them past the record number of consecutive wins set by Warwick Armstrong's Australians in 1920–21, a record the West Indies had equalled when they beat England by five Test matches to nil in the summer of 1984.

Lloyd praised his bowlers but said that some of his batsmen had not got going, and after the first day's play he had ordered a special net. It was another indication of the professionalism which was to devastate the Australians at Brisbane in the second Test.

Garner turned out to be the main destroyer when Australia batted first in this match. His four wickets for 67 runs helped reduce Australia to a first-innings total of 175. The West Indies reply was built around a magnificent century by Lloyd, made after he had faced only 120 deliveries. It was his 19th Test century and, with support from Richardson, the West Indies reached 424. There was never the slightest indication that the Australians would make a real fight of the match, and although their first-wicket partnership put on 88 there was a regular procession thereafter, Marshall taking five wickets for 82 runs and Holding chipping in with 4 for 92.

The match ended in considerable drama as the hapless Australian captain Kim Hughes, who had been steamrollered by the might of the West Indies, announced to a crowded post-match press conference that he was giving up the captaincy 'in the interests of Australian cricket'.

Poor Kim Hughes, criticised by former colleagues when he was captain, was pilloried by all and sundry for the manner of his departure. What seemed to have worried Australian supporters even more than the fact that their team was leaderless was the sight of their Test captain giving up his job in tears. The macho image of Australian sport has no place for the unduly lachrymose.

Lloyd had some sympathy for Hughes but felt that he should have stayed in the job and fought to redeem his reputation, even as Lloyd himself had done after a five-one drubbing on his first tour to Australia as West Indies captain. That was a measure of Clive Lloyd. The professional setbacks are to be put aside. The job's the thing.

Given all the drama at the end of the second Test, it would have been surprising if the Australians under their new captain Allan Border had managed to turn the tables on the West Indies in the third Test at Adelaide.

Lloyd won the toss and the West Indies made 356 in their first innings. The captain himself scored 78; only Greenidge, who made 95, did better. Wicket-keeper Dujon was out for 77 and the ever-reliable Gomes for 60.

The hero of the Australian attack was Lawson, whose tireless efforts brought him a haul of eight wickets for 112 runs. But Lawson's magnificence was not backed up by Australia's batting. Malcolm Marshall, as he had done twice before in the series, went through the Australian batting. He took five wickets for 69 runs, only Kepler Wessels with 98 offering any real resistance as Australia's innings folded for 284, 72 runs behind their opponents' score.

A fine century by Larry Gomes gave the West Indies a secure foundation when they batted a second time, although no other batsman save Desmond Haynes, who made 50, really got going. The great Viv Richards again failed to make any impression on the proceedings. Even so, Lloyd was able to declare his second innings closed at 292 with seven wickets down, setting Border's team 364 runs to make to save the game.

Australia's attempt to reach the target can only be described as dismal. Once again Marshall proved to be the architect of their destruction. Dyson and the resolute Wessels, who had been badly bruised by the West Indian fast bowlers when he batted in the first innings, put on 22 for the first wicket before Dyson played half forward to a ball which kept low and was out leg-before. Marshall had struck the first vital blow. Allan Border seemed to be hitting the ball well and had taken his own score to 18 and his side to 70 when he pushed at a brute of a delivery from Marshall, which pitched on middle stump and knocked back his offstump. The hapless Hughes was never allowed to settle or redeem anything of his lost honour. He played inside the line of a beautiful delivery from Marshall and was comprehensively bowled for 2. Australia were three wickets down for 78 and tumbling to disaster. A brilliant diving catch at second-slip by Roger Harper accounted for Boon when he had made only 9, and then Harper took the wickets of Wessels for 70 and Rixon for 19. Australia were suddenly without hope at 150 for 6. After that Marshall had Lawson caught behind, Harper bowled Rodney Hogg, and Marshall knocked back Terry Alderman's middle stump to return figures of 5 for 38 and to take his tenth wicket in the match. Australia, dismissed for 173, had lost the Adelaide Test by 191 runs and the West Indies had won the series.

It was their eleventh win in successive Tests, and Lloyd's team had now gone 27 Tests without defeat, beating England's run of 26 matches under Ray Illingworth between 1968 and 1971.

After such a convincing performance in Adelaide, the West Indies appeared to go on the defensive in the fourth Test in Melbourne. Lloyd again had first use of the wicket and his side scored impressively to make 479. Viv Richards returned to form with a devastating double century.

The Australians in their reply could only make 296, and when at the end of the fourth day the West Indies had further enhanced their position by making 163 for the loss of five wickets, few observers felt that Lloyd would choose to bat on into the fifth day. At stumps on day four, the West Indies were 346 runs ahead, with only three full sessions of play left.

But Lloyd decided to bat for just under half an hour more on the final day, and at stumps, when Australia were hanging on by the slenderest of threads with eight wickets down and only 198 runs on the board, the twenty-four minutes used up by the West Indies batsmen when play began might have been more appreciated by their bowlers. Time had run out for the West Indies.

Lloyd's decision to continue batting on the final day, when his team held such an advantage over a shellshocked Australian team, was surprising to say the least. His explanation was that he wanted to put the match beyond Australia's reach. He felt that although the wicket had been unpredictable, batsmen who weren't reckless could hang around for a long time, and possibly get the runs.

What seemed more likely was that the usually aggressive West Indian captain was still haunted by the memory of the Test match against India in Port of Spain in April 1976. He had won the series in the previous game and saw no reason to take unnecessary risks. His team had continued under his leadership to create cricket history despite the drawn fourth Test; their unbeaten run had been extended to 28 matches.

But Lloyd's fear may have given the new Australian captain hope. Even as his team held on grimly for a draw in Melbourne, there had been some encouraging signs for Allan Border. The chief of these had been the batting of the new Australian opener, Andrew Hilditch. He was the mainstay of Australia's second innings with an excellent score of 113. One week later in Sydney, Border was to have good reason to praise some other 'new faces' in his side.

The Australians gained a significant advantage at the start of the fifth Test in Sydney when Border won the toss and chose to bat. He later admitted that he had been in something of a panic when he called correctly, but he followed the advice of the New South Wales players in his team. It proved a match-winning decision. Led by the stout-hearted Wessels, who bore with the greatest fortitude everything the

West Indies pace men could throw at him to make 173, Australia's batting reached its maturity for the first time in the series. Border's contribution was a splendid 69 in a first-innings tally of 471 for 9 declared. The West Indies most successful bowler was Holding, who took 3 for 74. By West Indian standards their pace bowlers had taken a pasting. It was an ominous sign, but worse was to follow. The team whose success had been built around fast bowlers were about to be bamboozled by spin. Legspinner Bob Holland, aged 38 and playing in only his third Test, took six West Indian wickets for 54 runs and reduced the West Indies reply to a paltry 163. Only Desmond Haynes batted with anything resembling confidence, and he could only make 34.

Following on, an indignity which had become a totally strange experience to West Indian Test teams, the West Indies soon lost Haynes and ended the third day of the match on an unhappy 31 for 1.

The fourth day was a sad end to Clive Lloyd's leadership of the West Indies side. Before the match he had said that it would be his last Test, and during the game itself he affirmed that he had made up his mind to 'call it a day'.

Resuming their second innings on day four, the West Indies soon lost Gomes to the indefatigable Lawson for 8. Then, with the score on 46, Greenidge tried to cut Holland and was bowled for 12. Viv Richards and his fellow Antiguan team-mate put on a gritty 47 before Richardson was snapped up close to the wicket off slow left-armer Bennett for 26.

Walking out to bat for the West Indies for the last time, Clive Lloyd was loudly cheered all the way to the middle. He appeared to have all the answers to the spin attack which had so humbled his other batsmen. He drove fiercely through mid-off, danced down the track to hoist one half-volley over the boundary ropes for six, and hit the ball through the onside field with all the pugnacity of old. He and Richards put on 50 in better than even time and their partnership had realised 60 when Richards was fooled by Murray Bennett's 'arm ball' and a delivery he thought he could cut at, outside offstump, came back to take his middle stump. He had made a brave 58.

Lloyd had scored a stylish and defiant 72 when he drove at fast bowler Craig McDermott and was caught by Border in the covers. The West Indies were 231 for 7 and slipping inexorably to their first defeat in 29 Tests. Malcolm Marshall held out for as long as he had partners, but in the end they ran out leaving him undefeated with 32 and the West Indies an innings and 55 runs in arrears. Holland had taken four wickets, making his haul for the match ten. Clive Lloyd, who had been cheered all the way to the wicket, was given a standing ovation as he walked back to the pavilion.

In Australia's moment of glory Prime Minister Bob Hawke presented the Frank Worrell Trophy to Lloyd for winning the series, and the West Indian captain settled down to his farewell interviews and the world of cricket to tributes to one of the greatest captains of all time.

He reflected that he had won his first Test match as captain, so that perhaps there was some peculiar balance at the end of his career in that he had lost his last. He admitted that he would miss the rigours of Test cricket, but felt that the time had at last come to do something else.

Months before Lloyd decided that the Sydney Test match in January 1985 was to be his last, the Indian captain Sunil Gavaskar, who had once criticised Lloyd's style of leadership, had written a fitting tribute to a brilliant player and captain. In his book *Idols* Gavaskar wrote: 'Clive, I just hope you keep on playing. We cricketers and the cricket lovers need you more than you think.'

On the day Lloyd played his last innings for the West Indies in a Test match, Gavaskar was leading India against England in Calcutta. From there the Lancashire and England player Graeme Fowler, who had suffered at the hands of Lloyd's pace bowlers during the summer of 1984, was still able to say this about the West Indies captain:

He's been a hard man as captain. Despite his genial personality, he was tough. He has always been a great disciplinarian, on the field and off the field. That, I think, is the main reason he has been able to mould the West Indies into such a fine side. I have no doubt that the West Indies will miss this great player and successful captain.

One last point needs to be made about Clive Lloyd's leadership of the West Indies team. The same tactics which earned Lloyd and his fast bowlers such international disfavour made them heroes in the eyes of their own people – those who now live in England and those cricket fanatics back in the West Indies.

Anyone who doubts this should remind himself of the scenes of West Indian jubilation at the conclusion of the 1984 'blackwash' of England at Kennington Oval in South London. The same Lloyd philosophy which elicited such trenchant criticism in England was hailed in the Caribbean as having brought about a renaissance in the West Indian game.

Those who find it difficult to understand why Clive Lloyd and his quartet of pace bowlers appeared so contemptuously immune to continual carping about short-pitched bowling and slow over-rates, need to remind themselves that those criticisms are totally dismissed in the West Indies. Clive Lloyd was not acting on his own. His authority derived from West Indian cricket administrators who could ill afford to ignore success or be critical of the means by which that success had been achieved, and from an ultra-critical West Indian public who demand nothing less and who insist that failure be penalised. Their attitude is complicated by history. Their outlook has much more to do with politics than with cricket.

In common with a number of other small, developing countries in the world, the West Indian perception of history is that they have always been the victims of exploitation by the big powers. Their economies were adapted, sometimes artificially, to produce what the colonial powers wanted. They were in a very real sense the hewers of wood and drawers of water. And even though, since those dark days, they have achieved political independence, it is still the belief in some West Indian islands that attempts are continually being made by the big powers in international forums like the United Nations to demean their success and to challenge and undermine their independence.

In the aggression of West Indies cricket, the islands have found some minimal redress. Their record here is plain for all to see. It is undeniable. And West Indians are not easily dissuaded from the view that criticisms of their cricket merely represent another attempt to discredit them at all costs. That is why they will not be moved.

Anyone who finds this far-fetched should study closely the reaction of Malcolm Marshall or Michael Holding to warnings from umpires about short-pitched bowling. They barely acknowledge these and stroll back to their marks with a kind of studied disdain. And they should remember carefully the dismissive attitude of Holding's and Marshall's captain, Clive Lloyd, at first-slip. The West Indian attitude is not meant to be insolent. It is rather a statement that they will not be prevented from playing the game the way they believe they must play to win. They will not be frightened into playing it any other way. It is almost as though they echo what James Baldwin wrote about the revolution in America from a tacit acceptance of racism by some blacks to the undisguised advocacy of more militant solutions: 'That particular aspect of our journey is behind us. The secret is out. We are men.'

Lloyd himself came closest to saying exactly this on his last tour of

Australia in 1984–85, when after the West Indies had won the first three Test matches criticisms continued about the manner in which they had approached the games.

Lloyd said:

We are furious at the constant sniping at us from all over the world. Critics are trying to degrade our excellence and our achievements. That is the real reason behind statements that we bowl too many bouncers and that we were the first to start bowling short-pitched deliveries at tailend batsmen. We didn't of course. The Australians started that. But it's all being said falsely by people who wish to deny us our rightful title as the best team around. It really makes me hopping mad. For the rest of the series, we are determined to hit the Australians with everything we have.

No one would deny that as West Indian captain from 1974 to January 1985 Clive Lloyd gave the job everything he had. He asks for no other judgement of his stewardship.

Writing in the *Guardian*, John Arlott, cricket commentator emeritus, recorded this tribute to Lloyd:

He ambled, apparently abstractedly, in the field, sun-hat brim folded up like some amiable Paddington Bear, but upon the cue of a stroke played near him he leapt like some great cat into explosive action . . . he returned [the ball] with a whip of a mighty right arm, or off-balance with a strikingly accurate palm push.

Of Lloyd's batting Arlott wrote:

Physically his great reach enabled him to drive 'on the up' deliveries to which ordinary men would play back. This combination of reach, enormous strength, natural timing and instinctive attacking urge made him one of the most effective and powerful controlled hitters the game has known.

In Arlott's view:

Lloyd's captaincy has been marked by dignity; firm, unfussy discipline; and cool, realistic strategy. Some among his opponents have criticised him for the ruthless use of his mighty battery of fast bowlers. He, in typically relaxed fashion, has indicated that given the sharpest of cricketing weapons, he will employ it and that the matter of intimidatory bowling is one for the decision of the umpires.

CHAPTER THIRTEEN
Into the Unknown

The day after Clive Lloyd played his last innings for the West Indies in a full Test match, newspapers throughout the cricketing world saluted a hero. They all praised his record as captain in 74 Tests (nearly double the previous record of Peter May), beaten in only two of his 18 series, with an unprecedented sequence of 11 successive victories and 27 successive Tests without defeat, and a batting average of more than 50 as captain.

Commentators, even those critical of his dependence on fast bowling as the main instrument of his success, praised the awesome power of his batting, his wonderfully controlled temperament in the heat of the toughest battle, and his brilliance as cover fielder before his knees forced him to limit his attentions to first-slip.

The writer in *The Times* felt that despite the overuse of the word 'great' no other could adequately describe Clive Hubert Lloyd. One headline read: 'Exit the Bear from the world's stage.' Another: 'A giant lopes off into the sunset.' The departure of Lloyd the colossus from the stage of international cricket, and the many tributes to his astonishing success, helped to obscure a lively debate about the fate of the West Indies team after Lloyd.

Lloyd himself put the matter beyond question when immediately after the final Test against the Australians in Sydney in the opening week of 1985 he announced that his vice-captain Viv Richards would take over as West Indies captain for the remainder of the tour. This meant that Richards led the team in the triangular World Series Cup matches against the other participants, Australia and Sri Lanka. But Lloyd's announcement helped to disguise the heart-searching among the West Indian cricket authorities as to whether Richards was the most suitable candidate to succeed him.

This question can only be properly considered from two standpoints – those of Richards himself and of the Board. Richards takes up the leadership of the West Indies side with something of a chip on his shoulder. He has come to believe that there has been something approaching a conspiracy to keep him from taking up the job. The fact that Lloyd finally decided to go after the Sydney Test in January 1985, and to pass the mantle over to him, would not in itself have calmed his fears.

They are not without justification.

The seeds of Richards' fears were sown after India beat the West Indies to win the Prudential World Cup in 1983, when Clive Lloyd announced that he was giving up the captaincy. Lloyd went further. He took it for granted, and publicly said so, that he would hand over the leadership of the team to the man who had been his deputy for some five years, Viv Richards. But the manager of that touring West Indies team, Clyde Walcott, reproached Lloyd for assuming that the captaincy of the West Indies was in his gift. Walcott had let the secret out of the bag. The West Indies had not yet decided whether Richards should be Lloyd's successor. Walcott's comment to Lloyd about the captaincy was overheard by Richards, and from that moment on his suspicions were raised.

The next event in the saga confirmed in Richards' mind at least that there was 'a conspiracy' to deny him of what towards the end of the 1984 West Indies tour of England he came to call his 'rights'. Believing that Lloyd's decision to give up the captaincy had been made in the trauma of having lost the World Cup to India, long regarded as the minnows of the international game, the West Indies Board asked Lloyd to think again. When he did decide to carry on as captain, he tried to warn Richards of his change of heart. His call never found his vice-captain and Richards heard the news on early morning radio and from his team-mates at the Somerset ground at Taunton.

For a long time after that, Richards seemed quite prepared to nurture his disappointment in stoic and dignified silence. In interviews he repeatedly praised 'Clive's leadership of the team' and always sought to convince his interlocutors that his thoughts were firmly fixed on making runs for his side and not on the captaincy of the West Indies. In one interview he even averred that should he not be given the job when Lloyd retired he would swallow his hurt, put his head down and concentrate on what he does best – destroying the morale of bowlers with his flashing sword. But then, having reflected on the matter more deeply, he came round to the belief that the real reason for Lloyd's reappointment was an attempt to deprive him of the chance to lead the West Indies. Richards even lost sympathy with Lloyd's stated reason for returning – the claim that he had been persuaded to do so by the entreaties of the West Indies Board.

If a man says he's quitting [said Richards] and if he really means it, then that's that; no one can persuade him to come back. That's impossible. There must be some other reason why he does it. What am I to believe? All I am demanding now is my rights. I am West Indies vice-captain, I have done the job and naturally I want to be captain. That's all there is to it. That is my right. No one can deny me my rights. If I'm denied what's rightfully mine, then there'll be trouble.

Richard's uncertainty about what the Board intended was not helped by the fact that during the 1984 West Indies tour of England he had to tolerate endless speculation in the British sporting press about who would succeed Lloyd. That hurt, because as far as he was concerned the matter should have been a foregone conclusion. There had been murmurs during the West Indies tour of India in 1983 that Jeffrey Dujon, the wicket-keeper batsman 'showed all the qualities of a future West Indies captain'.

Back in England in 1984 a new name surfaced. Roger Harper, the Guyanese offspinner, lower-order batsman and superb close-to-the-wicket fieldsman, was also mentioned as a possible West Indian captain of the future. Advocates of Harper's claim talked about how competently he had led the young West Indies team to England some years before, and about his excellent 'tour report' which apparently made a lasting impression on the Board.

What must have worried Richards more than anything else was the fact that press speculation had the effect of creating the belief that the captaincy issue had not been settled, that it was still a wide-open affair. The name Larry Gomes cropped up later in 1984, and Gordon Greenidge, in denying that he would ever be chosen to lead the West Indies, never gave any hint that he felt the question had been decided.

The West Indies Board has always viewed the problem of Lloyd's successor as one rooted in the personalities of the two men, Lloyd and Richards. Clive Lloyd has always managed to create the impression that he is an easygoing character. He managed to mask his fiercely competitive streak beneath a quiet, sauntering, almost benevolent appearance. There is hardly an abrasive side to his nature. In the face of the most heated controversies his voice is hardly ever raised. His positions are stated firmly, even animatedly, but never with a great deal of shouting or handwaving. He could be stubborn, at times intransigent and curtly dismissive of arguments with which he did not agree. But seldom during his years as a player or as a captain did he openly display ill temper. Annoyed, he kept his emotions firmly under control. Only those closest to him would suspect things were wrong as he sank deeper into brooding silence.

The Board would find Richards an entirely different proposition. Although he has learnt to curb his show of temper, it can still get the better of him. He will happily trade insults with the best or the worst. His fierce pride in what he has achieved for himself and his country Antigua makes him openly intolerant of anything he perceives as humbug. He is aggressive, but even more to the point he has a profound distrust of authority. He comes close to believing that authority, certainly of the kind wielded by the West Indies Board, simply gets in the way of true genius, stifles greatness and is not meant to help the players. He believes that he and authority have always been and will always be collision-bound.

He considers that most authority is out to demean him, to belittle what he has achieved, to make him less of a man, somehow to rob him of his pride and his dignity. Thus he hates being told what to do. He might easily interpret suggestions from the Board as attempts to make him do its bidding. Such a relationship between Richards and the governors of West Indian cricket could be turbulent. Since the Packer affair in effect ushered in an era of 'player power' in the West Indies, Richards is sure that the Board is not in touch with the contemporary realities of the game. Lloyd, having won his battle with the West Indian cricket authorities over the Packer business, felt sufficiently sure of himself to be able to treat with the Board on a new footing of mutual respect. He had won his battle; Richards might well feel that he is yet to win his.

Another point which may worry the Board is his unbending affection for his Rastafarian friends. He wears the movement's colours as a sweat band on his wrist and is deeply fond of the music associated with the movement (his favourite is Bob Marley's redemption song).

This worries the Board. And it has been frequently put to Richards that if his promotion to the captaincy of the West Indies team is to be assured, he should distance himself from his more unconventional friends. The subject came up as recently as early 1984, at the end of the Australian tour of the West Indies. On that occasion the hint came from none other than the President of the West Indies Board, Allan Rae, himself no hide-bound conservative.

Richards has remained adamant. So long as his private life does not affect his cricket, he will do as he pleases and retain the friends he has always had. He has said time and again that he will not be dictated to by anyone. The Board's worry, put simply, is that with Richards they will almost certainly lose the cosy relationship that has characterised their dealings with elder statesman Lloyd in the last few years.

The West Indies cricket authorities believe that Richards' prickly personality is a distinct disadvantage in a leader of men. Not only that. They also believe they have evidence to support the view that his impatience with others less accomplished than himself, his intolerance of the failings of his fellow players, might make for discomfort and ill-feeling in the team. The evidence cited in support of this contention is that one young West Indian player left the field in tears after he appeared to have been rounded on by the vice-captain for a minor misdemeanour. In the view of the people who run West Indies cricket, such an attitude by a possible captain of the team bodes ill for the future. And the captain's report after the West Indies 1983 tour of India would have included the observation that in Delhi, Richards, struggling to get runs and finding himself at the wrong end of a questionable umpiring decision, caused havoc in the dressing-room.

To complicate matters, West Indian 'politics' have entered the debate. Antiguans, and the Prime Minister and Richards' father and Andy Roberts are among them, have pressed their man's claim to the captaincy. They are supported by representatives of some of the smaller islands. The Richards' case is not so firmly supported in Barbados, Trinidad, Guyana and Jamaica. It will be a grave mistake to ignore the political dimension of the debate.

By his own description, Lloyd was 'thunderstruck' when he was appointed West Indies captain. Richards waited in the wings for a number of years. Like Othello he insists he has done 'the state some service and they know it'. He has served his apprenticeship and the job is now his by right. He is sure in his own mind he has *earned* it. That might make his approach slightly different from that of his predecessor.

And he will be very disappointed if he is not given a fair run at proving himself an able captain and first-class replacement for Lloyd. But that might not be as simple as it appears. West Indians have come to cherish certain feelings of invincibility about their cricket, and Clive Lloyd's reign as captain helped promote that view. Whereas the English love the happy amateur who loses with sporting dignity, winning is the only thing that matters to West Indians, and unless he produces quick results Richards might have some difficulty keeping his job.

Unlike an England captain who is responsible to a group of selectors, a West Indian captain has, in effect, different masters and detractors in almost every Test-playing country in the region. They may not all have a strictly 'statutory' involvement in administering the game, but they can be intolerant of shortcomings and scathing of failure.

To compound his problems, Richards will know that he is not the unanimous choice of all the islands. And those who did not want him to succeed Lloyd will be waiting to pounce. Leading a West Indies team can be a harshly unpleasant business. Those who doubt it must remind themselves how, for years, there was a running feud between the gentle-natured Lloyd and the Trinidadian cricket public.

A fresh debate has already started about the West Indies captaincy. Richards will not find a great deal of comfort in the fact that it has already been joined by no less a person than Sir Garfield Sobers. While Richards was struggling to find his form in the early part of the 1984–85 Australian tour, Sobers was telling television audiences in Trinidad that in his view Lloyd's successor should be Trinidadian Larry Gomes. It is always possible that Sobers, ever the thoughtful guest, was simply playing up to his hosts, saying what he thought Trinidadians would like to hear. Even if that is true, it means that there are other names being mentioned in other West Indian islands.

Lloyd gained the reputation of being something of a diplomat, cricket's unflappable elder statesman. Richards prefers straight talking to diplomacy. He is down-to-earth, honest and says what he thinks. To him, speaking one's mind far outweighs the virtues of diplomatic silence. He might find his West Indian critics equally blunt.

But the most difficult task facing Viv Richards will be the very simple one of filling the shoes of the master. Even for the greatest of players, and Richards must be counted among these, it represents a formidable task.

How does one follow the most successful captain in the history of the game? Will he be supported by his colleagues, who came to look on Clive Lloyd almost as the protector of their interests? And will he be given time by the West Indies Board to make his mark, or will they look for the first excuse to confirm their belief that perhaps Richards is not the man for the job after all?

The colossus has left the spotlight, but he has left his successor in the shadows.

APPENDIX
Clive Lloyd – Career Statistics

APPENDIX

Clive Lloyd – Career Statistics

Clive Lloyd's record as West Indies captain:

YEAR	OPPONENTS	MATCHES	WON	LOST	DRAWN
1974–75	India	5	3	2	0
1975	Pakistan	2	0	0	2
1975–76	Australia	6	1	5	0
1976	India	4	2	1	1
1976	England	5	3	0	2
1977	Pakistan	5	2	1	2
1978	Australia	2	2	0	0
1979–80	Australia	2	2	0	0
1980	New Zealand	3	0	1	2
1980	England	4	1	0	3
1980	Pakistan	4	1	0	3
1981	England	4	2	0	2
1981–82	Australia	3	1	1	1
1983	India	5	2	0	3
1983	India	6	3	0	3
1984	Australia	4	3	0	1
1984	England	5	5	0	0
1984–85	Australia	5	3	1	1
	TOTAL	74	36	12	26

Against each country:

	PLAYED	WON	LOST	DRAWN
Australia	22	12	7	3
England	18	11	0	7
India	20	10	3	7
New Zealand	3	0	1	2
Pakistan	11	3	1	7

Test match batting record

YEAR	OPPONENTS	MATCHES	INNINGS	N.O.	RUNS	HIGHEST SCORE	AV.	100S
1966–67	India	3	5	1	227	82	56.75	—
1968	England	5	9	2	369	118	52.71	2
1968–69	Australia	4	8	0	315	129	39.37	1
1969	New Zealand	3	5	0	65	44	13.00	—
1969	England	3	6	0	183	70	30.50	—
1971	India	5	10	0	295	64	29.50	—
1972	New Zealand	2	3	0	66	43	22.00	—
1973	Australia	3	6	1	297	178	59.50	1
1973	England	3	5	0	318	132	63.60	1
1974	England	5	7	1	147	52	24.50	—
1974–75	India	5	9	1	636	242*	79.50	2
1975	Pakistan	2	3	0	164	83	54.66	—
1975–76	Australia	6	11	1	469	149	46.90	2
1976	India	4	6	0	283	102	47.16	1
1976	England	5	9	0	296	84	32.88	—
1977	Pakistan	5	9	1	336	157	42.00	1
1978	Australia	2	2	0	128	86	64.00	—
1979–80	Australia	2	3	0	201	121	67.00	1
1980	New Zealand	3	6	0	103	42	17.16	—
1980	England	4	4	0	169	101	42.25	1
1980	Pakistan	4	6	1	106	37	21.20	—
1981	England	4	5	0	383	100	76.60	1
1981–82	Australia	3	6	1	275	77	55.00	—
1983	India	5	6	0	407	143	67.83	2
1983	India	6	8	2	496	161	82.66	2
1984	Australia	4	4	0	170	76	42.50	—
1984	England	5	6	1	255	71	51.00	—
1984–85	Australia	5	8	1	356	114	50.85	1
TOTAL		110	175	14	7515	242*	46.67	19

Bowling record: 1710 balls, 621 runs, 10 wickets, average 62.10

Best bowling performance: 2 for 13 against England in Barbados in 1974

Fielding: 89 catches

Batting record:
as player: 36 matches, 64 innings, 5 not outs, 2282 runs, highest score 178, average 38.67, hundreds 5

as captain: 74 matches, 111 innings, 9 not outs, 5233 runs, 242* highest score, average 51.30, hundreds 14

Lancashire career figures

YEAR	MATCHES	INNINGS	N.O.	RUNS	HIGHEST SCORE	AV.	100S
1968	1	1	0	1	1	1.00	0
1969	10	15	1	554	99	39.57	0
1970	18	28	2	1203	163	46.26	3
1971	22	33	4	1124	217	38.75	2
1972	18	26	4	895	181	40.68	3
1973	6	10	1	271	66	30.11	0
1974	20	31	8	1458	178	63.39	4
1975	18	27	4	1423	167	61.86	6
1976	DID NOT PLAY						
1977	5	3	1	164	95	82.00	0
1978	21	36	6	1116	120	37.20	4
1979	16	22	4	880	104	48.88	3
1980	18	31	2	1324	145	45.65	1
1981	18	31	0	1340	101	44.66	1
1982	21	29	2	1135	100	42.03	1
1983	11	16	1	447	86	29.80	0
1984	DID NOT PLAY						

Index

Index

Notes: Test match series are entered under the name of the home side. Clive Lloyd is abbreviated to CL.

Abbas, Zaheer 95
Alam, Intikhab 50
Alderman, Terry 150
Alexander, Gerry 32, 34, 66, 130
Ali, Imtiaz 83
Allan, David 22
Allen, Gubby 27, 76
Allott, Paul 123, 124
Antigua 161
Archer, Ronald 30
Arlott, John 155
Amarnath, Mohinder 84, 85
Armstrong, Warwick 149
Arnold, Geoff 61
Atkinson, Denis 29–31
Australia 10, 130, 157; World Cup matches 75–7, 101, 102
Australia v. England (1982–83) 137
Australia v. West Indies: (1960) 36; (1968–69) 40–45; (1975–76) 78–82, 107–8, 134; (1979–80) 97; (1981–82) 130; (1984–85) 146–53

Bacchus, F. 101
Bailey, Trevor 135
Baldwin, James 154
Baptiste, Eldine 111, 115, 116, 120, 123, 147
Barlow, Eddie 50
Barrington, Ken 33
Bedi, B. S. 83
Benaud, Richie 30, 79, 130, 131, 147
Bennett, Murray 152
Bird, Dickie 112, 116
'bird tickets' 15–16
Blofeld, Henry xiii, 40, 44
Bond, Jackie xi, 71, 72
Boon, Timothy 150
Booth, Howard 65
Borde, C. G. 24
Border, Allan 9, 149, 150, 151, 152

Botham, Ian 97, 99, 113–24 *passim*, 128–9
bowling: fast 78–82, 84, 86–7, 105–12, 127, 135–6, 146–8, 153, 156; short-pitched 112, 114–15, 154; spin 82–4
Boyce, K. D. 81
Boycott, Geoffrey 2, 46, 63, 96–7, 116
Bradman, Donald 77, 116, 122, 142
Brearley, Mike 95, 96, 97, 100, 128, 134
Brittenden, R. T. 97–8
Broad, Chris 119, 120, 123, 125
Burgess, M. G. 95
Burnham, Forbes 58, 60
Butcher, Basil 20, 22, 23, 24, 26, 37, 39, 46, 48, 142
Bynoe, Robin 20, 24, 31

Camacho, George 18
Camacho, Steve 37, 46
Capildeo, Rudranath 51
captaincy, West Indies 2, 29–36, 40–45
Cardus, Neville xii, 11, 62, 67–8
Carew, Joey 41, 55
Carrick, Phil 100
Challenge Newspaper 59
Chandrasekar, B. S. 24, 25, 41, 83
Chappell, Greg 4, 78, 116
Chappell, Ian 41, 42, 60, 75, 76, 77, 78, 79, 82, 147–8
Christiani, Robert 15, 18
Close, Brian 27, 38, 39, 88, 105, 106, 135
coaching 64
Compton, Denis 77, 112, 116
Constantine, Learie xii, 27, 29, 33, 35, 62, 67–8, 141
Cosier, Gary 79, 81–2
County championship, English (1970) 49–50

Cowdrey, Colin 31, 37, 39, 45–6, 106, 116, 135
Cozier, Tony xiii, 37, 60, 86–7
Croft, Colin 7, 95, 97, 98, 99
Cumberbatch, Colin xiii

Daniel, Wayne 87, 88
Davis, Charlie 46, 59
Davis, Winston 101, 125
Demerara Cricket Club 15, 17–19
De Peiza, Clairmonte 49
Derbyshire 73
Dev, Kapil 120
Dexter, Ted 33, 135
Downton, Paul 119
Dujon, Jeff 120, 124, 148, 149, 159
Durani, S. A. 24
Dyson, John 150

Ealham, Allan 73
Edmonds, Phil 73
Edrich, John 39, 88, 105
Emburey, John 138
Engineer, Farouk 50, 71
England 130; overseas players in 129; World Cup matches 96–7
England v. Rest of the World (1970) 50
England v. West Indies: (1950) 27; (1957) 29, 31–2; (1963) 36; (1966) 21–2; (1969) 45–8; (1973) 61, 64; (1976) 86–8; (1980) 99
England v. West Indies (1984) 105–29, 153, 158, 159; at Edgbaston 114–18; at Lord's 119–22; at Headingley 123–4; at Old Trafford 124–5
English wickets 126–7
Evans, Godfrey 135

Fagg, Arthur 63
Fletcher, Keith 128
Fowler, Graeme 110, 114, 116, 119, 120, 122, 123, 124, 125, 153
Fredericks, Roy 46, 76, 78, 79, 80, 83, 87
Frith, David xiii, 115

Gaekwad, Anshuman 84, 85
Garner, Joel 9, 10, 11, 95, 97, 99, 101, 111, 113, 114, 116, 120, 123, 147, 148, 149

Gaskin, Berkeley 19, 41
Gatting, Mike 119, 121
Gavaskar, Sunil xiii, 54, 55, 83, 84–5, 109, 116, 135–6, 153
Geddes Grant and Harrison Line Trophy 1
Gibbs, Lance 1, 15, 19, 22, 26, 38, 50, 82, 125, 142
Gibbs, Oscar 143
Gilchrist, Roy 32–3
Gillette Cup 49, 56, 57, 67, 68–9, 71–2, 73, 99–100
Gilmour, Gary 78
Glamorgan 48, 88–9
Gleeson, John 41
Gloucester 68–9
Goddard, John 31, 130
Gomes, Larry 101, 114, 115, 119, 120, 122, 123, 124, 136, 148, 149, 150, 152, 159, 162
Gooch, Graham 96, 97, 138
Gover, Alf xi
Gower, David xiii, 109, 112, 114, 115, 116, 119, 120, 123, 124; captaincy and 128–9; on CL 136–7
Grant, George 131
Graveney, Tom xi, 39, 62, 135
Greenidge, Gordon 10, 76, 80, 87, 95, 96, 98, 101, 102, 103, 114, 115, 119, 120, 132, 135, 147, 149, 152, 159; double centuries 122, 124–5; on CL 133–4
Greig, Tony 73, 86, 134
Griffith, Charlie 20, 22, 24, 26, 37–8, 40, 46
Guyana 1, 13, 51, 58, 99
Guyana v. Barbados (1966) 19–20

Hadlee, Walter 98
Hall, Mervyn xiii
Hall, Wes 11, 22, 24, 26, 40, 46, 49, 58–9
Hammond, Walter 116, 122
Hampshire, John 46
Harper, Roger 116, 120, 123, 124, 125, 135, 136, 150, 159
Harper, Rudolph 17
Harvey, Neil 30
Haslingden 49
Hawke, Bob 153
Hayes, Frank 73, 100

Haynes, Desmond 7, 8, 9, 10, 94, 95, 96, 101, 102, 114, 115, 119, 120, 122, 150, 152
Headley, George 35, 49, 87
Hector, Colin 15
helmets 89
Hendrick, Michael 97
Hendricks, Jackie 22, 105
Heron, Colin 18
Hilditch, Andrew 151
Hogg, Rodney 147
Holder, Vanburn 74, 81, 84
Holding, Michael 9, 81–8 passim, 95, 97, 98, 99, 111, 115, 116, 123, 124, 147, 148, 149, 152, 154
Holford, David 22, 25
Holland, Bob 152
Holt, J. K. 49
Hookes, David 4, 9, 102
Hughes, Kim 102, 148, 150
Hunte, Conrad 20, 22, 24, 25, 26, 37
Hutton, Len 28, 116

Illingworth, Ray 45, 46, 150
Imran Khan 95, 120
India: World Cup matches 95, 101, 102, 158
India v. West Indies: (1957) 32; (1966–67) 22–6; (1974–75) 66–7; (1983) 2, 102–4
Iqbal, Asif 95

Jackman, Robin 68, 99
Jamaica v. Guyana (1966) 20
James, C. L. R. xiii, 14, 29, 32, 34, 35
Jessop, G. L. 130
John Player League 49
Johnson, Graham 72
Julien, Bernard 80, 81, 83, 107

Kallicharran, Alvin 8, 61, 75–6, 78, 81, 83, 96, 99, 107, 138, 142
Kanhai, Rohan 1, 20–26 passim, 37, 41, 46, 50, 52, 53–4, 77, 106, 142; captaincy 58–61, 63–4
Kennedy, Andrew 73, 100
Kent 50, 72–3
King, Collis 96, 97
Kirmani, S. 85
Knott, Alan 37, 106

Laker, Jim 69, 120, 135
Lal, Madan 83, 85
Lamb, Allan 115, 119, 122, 123, 125
Lancashire 49–50, 64, 65, 67–73; Gillette Cup 49–50, 56, 57, 67, 100
Lancashire League 49
Larkins, Wayne 96, 97
Larwood, Harold 110
Lashley, Patrick 22
Lawry, Bill 41, 42, 43
Lawson, Geoff 147, 150, 152
Lever, Peter 72
Lewis, Tony 146
Lillee, Dennis 4, 78, 79, 80, 81, 86, 89, 107, 108
Lloyd, Andy 114
Lloyd, Barry 89, 96
Lloyd, Clive: batting 39, 47, 68, 73, 104, 115–16, 130, 155; bowling 70; captaincy of West Indies 2, 7–8, 11–12, 36, 56, 63–5, 80, 130–42, 155–6, 157; career statistics 163–5; cartilage operation 70; controversy and 2–3; damages awarded against Melbourne Age 10; double century record 88–9; early life in Guyana 14–18; fielding 15–16, 21, 70, 144; first-class début 19; Gillette cup and 99–100; highest score 66–7; injury 56, 144; left out of 1966 England tour 21; personality 159; physical fitness 16–17; school cricket 17; sports consultancy 145; tributes to 11; World Series and 90–94
Lloyd, David xi, 64, 67, 68, 100
Lloyd, Waveney xi, 142–5
Loader, Peter 135
Lock, Graham 135

McCabe, Stanley 77
McCombie, Jock xii
McDermott, Craig 152
McDonald, Colin 30
McKenzie, Graham 42
McMorris, Easton 22
Madray, Ivan 142
Majid Khan 95
Mankad, Ashok 54, 120
Manley, Michael 11
Marlar, Robin 105
Marsh, Rodney 79, 146–8

Marshall, Malcolm 9, 10, 99, 111, 114–12 *passim*, 132, 147, 148, 149, 150, 152, 154
Massie, Robert 120
May, Peter 31, 134, 157
Melbourne Age 10
Meyer, Barrie 120
Middlesex 67, 68, 73, 100
Miller, Geoffrey 113
Miller, Keith 30, 35
Mohammed, Mushtaq 50
Murray, Deryck 5–6, 7, 8, 40, 50, 67, 74–5, 78, 82, 94
Murray, Lance 5–6
Murray, 'Sonny' 6

Naipaul, V. S. 14
Nawaz, Safraz 95
Nazar, Mudassar 95
New Zealand: World Cup matches 95
New Zealand v. India (1956) 30–31
New Zealand v. West Indies: (1968–69) 43–5; (1980) 97–9
Noble, M. A. 128
Noble, Thelma 143
Norville, Don 43
Nurse, Seymour 20, 22, 23, 26, 37, 46

Old, Chris 97, 100
over rates 106, 110–11, 154

Packer, Kerry 65 *see also* World Series Cricket
Padmore, Albert 83
Pairaudeau, Bruce 30
Pakistan 131; World Cup matches 74–5, 95, 102
Parks, James 39
Pascoe, Lenny 4
Patel, Brijesh 83, 84, 85
Patterson, Patrick 71
Phillips, R. B. 10
Pierre, Lance 56
Pocock, Pat 39
Prasanna, Erapalli 53, 83
Pringle, Derek 113, 115, 121, 123
Procter, Mike 50, 68–9
professionalism 55, 65, 127–8, 131
Prudential World Cup (1983) 158

Rackemann, Carl 9, 147

Rae, Allan 11, 28, 160
Raja, Wasim 75
Ramadhin, Sonny 28, 32, 51
Randall, Derek 97, 114, 116
Rastafarianism 160
Redpath, Ian 79, 81
Rhodesia 53
Richards, Barry 50
Richards, Viv 9, 76, 80, 83, 86, 87, 95–103 *passim*, 114, 115, 119–20, 123, 132, 136, 147, 150, 151, 152; batting 112–13, 115; captaincy and 135, 157–62; personality 160–61
Richardson, Ritchie 9, 149, 152
Ritchie, G. M. 10
Rixon, S. J. 150
Roberts, Andy 74–5, 79, 81, 83, 87, 88, 95, 99, 101, 103
Robbins' XI, Derrick 49
Rowe, Lawrence 78, 80, 89

Sardesai, Dilip 53, 54
Selvey, Mike 87
Shastri, Ravi 102
Shell Shield 1, 99, 136
Shepherd, John 50
Shuttleworth, Kenneth 72
Simmons, Jack xi, 69–70, 71, 73, 145
Simpson, Bobby 4
Singh, Charan 33
Small, Milton 120, 121
Smith, M. J. K. 33
Snow, John 39, 61
Sobers, Gary 1, 2, 19–26 *passim*, 46, 50, 54, 55, 60, 142, 162; captaincy and 36–8, 40–45, 52–3, 56, 57, 62–3, 130, 131
Solkar, Eknath 53, 54, 55
Solomon, Joe 20, 142
Somerset 48
South Africa 99, 138–41
Sri Lanka 74, 157
Statham, Brian 33, 135
Stollmeyer, Jeffrey 6, 29, 30, 34–5, 76, 94
Sussex 71–2
Sutcliffe, Herbert 107
Swanton, E. W. 34–5, 72, 130, 138

Tayfield, Hugh 120
Taylor, Bob 2, 97

Tennyson, Alfred 27
Terry, Paul 123, 125
Thomas, Lennie 18
Thomson, Jeff 78, 80, 81, 86, 107,
    108
Times, The 28, 157
Trinidad 1, 51, 52; CL and 59; Test
    matches in 54
Trollope, Anthony 13
Trueman, Fred 33, 135
Tyson, Frank 81, 110

umpiring 81–2, 97–8
Underwood, Derek 50

Valentine, Alfred 28
Vengsarkar, D. B. 85, 101
Venkataraghavan, S. 24, 83, 85
Viswanath, G. R. 83, 84, 95

Wadekar, Ajit 54, 56
Walcott, Clyde 29, 30, 31, 35, 47,
    158
'walking' 106
Walters, Doug 77
Warwickshire 72
Weekes, Everton 29, 30, 35
Wessels, Kepler 150, 152
West Indian cricket: batting 81;
    players' remuneration 139–40;
    professionalism of 26, 55, 65, 127–
    8, 131; team selection 1–2, 21, 59;
    World Series and 90–94
West Indian Federation 14, 28
West Indies 13; politics 28, 50–52;
    141, 154, 161; watching cricket in
    15–16; World Cup matches 74–7
West Indies Cricket Board 34, 154; CL
    honoured by 1; relations with

players 3, 92–4, 103–4, 160; World
    Series Cricket and 5–7, 92–4, 133
West Indies v. Australia (1955) 29–30;
    (1965) 19; (1973) 57–60; (1977–78)
    3–5, 8; (1981–82) 100–101; (1984)
    1–2, 8–11
West Indies v. England: (1948) 28;
    (1959–60) 33; (1967–68) 36–9, 106;
    (1974) 64; (1980) 99; (1981) 131
West Indies v. India: (1971) 52–6;
    (1976) 82–6, 108, 151; (1982–83)
    101
West Indies v. New Zealand (1971–72)
    56–7
West Indies v. Pakistan (1957–58) 32
Whitlam, Gough 58
Williams, Eric 29, 33, 35, 51
Willis, Bob xiii, 65, 88, 107–8, 115,
    116, 123, 127, 135, 137
Willis, Fred 18–19
Wiltshire, Colin 15
Windward and Leeward Islands v.
    Guyana (1966) 20–21
Wisden xiii, 43–4, 134–5
Wood, Barry 72, 73
Wood, Jack 144
Woolridge, Ian 146
World Cup: (1975) 73–7; (1979) 94–
    7; (1983) 101–2
World Series Cricket 3–8, 89, 90–94,
    131–3, 139, 143, 160
Worrell, Frank 1, 19, 23, 28, 29;
    captaincy and 30–36, 62, 130–31,
    133, 141
Wright, Norman 18

Yallop, Graham 102
Yorkshire 100

Zimbabwe 102